The School Business Administrator

Fourth Edition, 1999

By
Kenneth R. Stevenson, Ed.D.
Don I. Tharpe, Ed.D.

ASSOCIATION OF SCHOOL BUSINESS OFFICIALS INTERNATIONAL

The School Business Administrator by
Kenneth R. Stevenson, Ed.D. and
Don I. Tharpe, Ed.D.
Copyright © 1999, by the
Association of School Business Officials International

Printed in the United States of America.
Published by Association of School Business Officials International.
11401 North Shore Drive, Reston, VA 20190-4232
ISBN No. 0-910-170-77-0

For more information or to purchase additional copies contact:
ASBO International
11401 North Shore Drive
Reston, VA 20190-4200 USA
703/ 478-0405

Table Of Contents

Introduction A Brief History of School Business Administrators *i*

Chapter 1 Who are the School Business Administrators: And what do they do? 1

Chapter 2 The School Business Administrator as Manager 13

Chapter 3 The Broad Responsibilities of School Business Administrators 24

Chapter 4 Typical Duties of the School Business Administrator 43

Chapter 5 What Should be the Preparation and Experience of the School Business Administrator? 57

Chapter 6 Procedures for Establishing or Restructuring a School Business Administrator's Position and Obtaining an Effective School Business Administrator 67

Chapter 7 Compensating the School Business Administrator 81

Chapter 8: The Legal Implications in School Business Administration 87

Chapter 9 Personal Characteristics of School Business Administrators and Code of Ethics 95

Chapter 10 Evaluating the School Business Administrator 103

Chapter 11 Emerging Issues, Problems, Challenges, and Concepts in School Business Administration 121

Bibliography 127

Introduction

A Brief History of School Business Administration

School business administration has existed since the beginning of the public school system in the United States, but the position of school business administrator was not considered as important at its inception as it is today. In early school systems, taxes or fees were collected for such purposes as paying teachers, keeping financial records, paying rents, and supplying fuel. At first, these duties usually were performed by local municipal officials and, later, by members or committees of local school boards. Even in some communities today, certain business aspects of public education are managed by municipal officials not directly associated with the schools. This is especially true in city school systems that are fiscally dependent upon a municipal government.

The need to the appoint a full-time school business administrator was first recognized in 1841 when the city council in Cleveland, Ohio, passed an ordinance providing for an "Acting Manager" of schools. It was his duty:

"to keep a set of books, in which he shall open an account for each teacher in the employ of the city, and to make an accurate entry of all moneys paid out... keep an accurate account to each school district, whether for teaching, or rent, or for other purposes...to provide fuel, take charge of the buildings and fixtures, and certify to the council the correctness of all accounts against the city for teaching, or for rents, fuel, repairs or fixtures on or about the school houses." (Hill, 1982)

It is interesting to note Cleveland did not appoint a superintendent of schools until 12 years later. Chicago and Philadelphia also appointed full-time school business managers several years before appointing their first superintendents of schools (Hill, 1982).

The importance of the school business administrator became increasingly apparent by the 1880s as schools became more complex. According to published proceedings of the National Education Association, at this time some professional educators called for the creation of a business division in city school districts.

During the late 19th and early 20th centuries, many local school trustees and superintendents came to recognize the importance of good business administration in their school systems. Accordingly, some school trustees employed a professionally trained educator as the superintendent of schools and a businessman as the business administrator. Both had equal status in the administrative hierarchy, and each was directly responsible to the board of education.

The concept of management in which the superintendent of schools and the school business administrator have equal status is referred to as "dual control." This system gained favor chiefly in New Jersey, Pennsylvania, and Canada. In most other sections of the United States, school trustees have adopted the "unit control" concept, which places complete administrative responsibility upon the superintendent of schools. The business administrator reports to the superintendent, while the trustees concentrate on policy development and determination.

By the turn of the century, the administration of business affairs in school systems began to assume a "tone" of professionalism. Leading school business administrators realized the importance of their duties, the effects of their services on education, and the need for defining specific aspects of their duties and responsibilities. In 1910, the National Association of School Accounting Officers was formed. It later changed its name to the National Association of School Accounting Business Officials, which subsequently became the National Association of School Business Officials of the United States and Canada. In 1986, the association adopted its current name, Association of School Business Officials International (ASBO International). With the advent and development of this association, school business administration has come to be recognized as a potent and positive force in American education (Hill, 1982).

In the early 1900s, literature on the various aspects of school business administration, particularly school finance and accounting, began to appear. Professor N. L. Engelhardt, Sr., of Teacher's College, Columbia University, was the first known instructor of a course in school business administration. The course was offered in the summer school session of 1926. In addition, Professor Engelhardt and his brother, Fred, produced a book entirely devoted to school business administration. Since that time, numerous books and articles have been published dealing with the multiple aspects of school administration (Hill, 1982).

Recognizing the need for definitive statements about this important area of school administration, representatives of ASBO, the American Association of School Administrators (AASA), and the National School Boards Association (NSBA) have periodically established basic definitions and descriptions of the work and role of the School Business Official and the School Business

Administrator. These have become the standard for the profession, and this revision continues these established definitions.

In 1964, ASBO took a giant step forward by establishing the concept of professional registration and formulating requirements for the professional registration of both School Business Officials and School Business Administrators. These qualifications and requirements have been updated periodically.

At the same time, ASBO has encouraged its affiliated state, provincial, regional and local leadership to work to establish certification and licensing requirements for entry level positions in the field by the states and provinces. New Jersey was one of the first to do so.

Most educators and the public now recognize that decisions about curriculum, school organization, and personnel are interdependent on decisions about finance, buildings, equipment, and supplies. By accepting the relationship between curriculum planning and schoolhouse construction, classroom activities and textbook procurement, budget planning and educational activities, and by classifying all as administrative responsibilities, school trustees have enhanced the professionalism of all school administrators, including the school business administrator.

School business administration is becoming increasingly important to the entire operation and concept of the school system. School business administrators must be trained and experienced in the field of education with emphasis on school business administration or trained and experienced in various phases of business with a knowledge of educational practices. The school business administrator is a crucial element in improving educational opportunity. The superintendent looks to this official to further educational efficiency and progress through the financial decisions made and the business functions directed by this officer.

Chapter 1

Who Are the School Business Administrators — And What Do They Do?

The Context of School Business Management

Public education is a multibillion dollar enterprise that is charged with the daunting responsibility of preparing students for the complex world of the 21st century. The expectations of parents, communities, policy makers, business leaders, and the taxpayer are myriad. They include everything from teaching a child to read to providing a safe learning and teaching environment, serving nutritional meals, and efficient management of public resources. Making the task even more challenging is the fact that schools and school systems operate under varying sets of statutory requirements and limitations enacted by individual states and provinces, as well as the national government. In addition, educational institutions usually must function within the still further distinctive policies and regulations established by local boards of education.

Obviously, the task of administering this vastly complex business of education requires professional leadership that is highly skilled and knowledgeable. One of the most vital members of the modern educational leadership team is the professional school business administrator. This person is often at the heart of the administration and management of one of the largest corporate endeavors in a community.

School business administrators provide leadership in operating hundreds of thousands of schools and tens of thousands of school districts throughout North America, as well as many other locations across the world. While the function remains the same, the exact role of the school business administrator performs within a given educational setting varies widely. In some districts, personnel responsible for the business aspects are directly responsible to and subordinate to the superintendent (unit control). In other districts, some or all of the business functions and services are independent of the superintendent (dual control).

District size also affects the role a school business administrator performs. In a small school system, the superintendent may be the only professional at the central office and must serve, among other duties, as the school business official. Large school districts often use a team approach to district-level leadership. Here, an individual professionally and specifically trained to manage the school system's business services works in concert with district-level leaders responsible for other operational aspects of the system.

While the school business administrator's job responsibilities are still focused on effective and efficient operation of the non-instructional aspects of a district, i.e. budgeting and accounting, the role has expanded substantially from even a few years ago. The modern school business administrator is viewed as an integral member of a team responsible for managing the educational process in a manner that educates students effectively while using limited resources efficiently. In this context, the school business administrator is as concerned about and interested in the academic success of children as he or she is in balancing the budget or construction management. And, the school business administrator, as a member of the team, is often held jointly accountable for the success of the school system in reaching its stated goals.

The Job Title

What job titles apply to school business professionals? The position responsible for the wide variety of functions in a school business operation is typically designated as "school business administrator." School business administrators—sometimes called managers—have been designated by the school board and/or the superintendent to accept general responsibility for the administration of the business affairs of a school district. Unless otherwise specified by local law or custom, the school business administrator reports to the school board through the superintendent of schools. Titles of school business administrators are typically global, representing the breadth of their responsibilities. Standard job titles include Associate Superintendent for Administration, Assistant Superintendent for Business, Executive Director of Support Services.

The term "school business official" usually refers to a professional with administrative responsibility for a specific aspect of the non-instructional operation of a school system, such as foodservice, finance, transportation, facilities, risk management, negotiations, etc. These positions typically report through the school business administrator, to the superintendent and school board. Titles of school business officials tend to be specific, such as Director of Finance, Transportation Supervisor, Risk Management Consultant, and Facilities Planning Specialist.

In 1964, ASBO further strengthened the use of such titles by authorizing its Board of Directors to develop suitable standards. "Registered School Business Administrator," "Registered School Business Official," and "Registered School Business Specialist" titles have now been awarded and attested by Certificates of Registry from the association. Many state, regional, and provincial groups have used these titles in seeking appropriate legislation for certification in their respective states. Registration requirements are presented at the end of this chapter.

Since the intent of this monograph is to address the broader context of school business management within the total operation of school districts, the focus will be on the school business administrator. However, the terms "school business official" and "school business administrator" are, in real life, often interchangeable. Many school business professionals have specific responsibilities but, at the same time, must manage or administer the broader function of the organization. In this monograph, the term "school business administrator" will generally be used to refer to professionals who have a combination of technical and managerial responsibilities related to the operation of the non-instructional function of a school system.

Job Responsibilities — An Overview

The position, responsibilities, and qualifications of the school business administrator have been evolving over many years and still developing. The concept of school business administration itself is constantly forming and reforming in much the same manner as is the concept of public school education. Thus, the responsibilities of the school business administrator in any given community must be described and understood in terms of local historic patterns, available staff, and the particular competencies of the individual. No two school business administrators have identical roles. Instead, experience suggests that a broad range of functions may be assigned to the school business administrator.

In some districts, one person may perform all the functions. In others, they will be shared among several professionals. Hence, the broad task definitions of school business management job responsibilities that follow may be assigned to one individual or to a management team—depending on the specific setting of the community, the number of students served, and the expertise of the district staff.

Two basic concepts serve as the foundation of effective management and operation for all school business administrators, however. These are the *Team Concept* and the *Service Concept*. Regardless of specific technical duties and responsibilities, these two concepts must be in place for a school business administrator to be successful.

The Team Concept

The school business administrator is a highly qualified member of the superintendent's cabinet and has multiple responsibilities to the superintendent, the school board, the schools, and the community. As the person in charge of most, if not all, non-instructional aspects of the local educational system, the school business administrator is directly and continuously responsible for managing resources, provision and care of facilities, transportation, foodservice, and other vital support functions that assist the superintendent and teachers in delivering the educational experiences deemed necessary by the community. In essence, the school business manager is an integral part of a district team that delivers quality education. School business administrators today are expected to be intimately involved in planning for and accomplishing the broadest goals of the school system.

In many school districts today, the school business manager is a member of the superintendent's cabinet, or top-level administrative advisory body. As a member of the front line team, the school business administrator provides direct input and advice to the superintendent on all major policy issues of the school district.

In the past, the school business function often was viewed as having little or no role to play in instructional issues. However, modern school systems have come to recognize that coordination and involvement of district-level support components are often critical elements in the success of educational initiatives. Thus, school business administrators have become an integral and indispensable part of the management team in most of school districts.

In fact, in many school districts the school business administrator is designated second in command, and has a title such as Deputy Superintendent. In this time of limited resources and high accountability, many communities look to the school business official for confirmation that proposed educational practices and changes are fiscally sound, economically feasible, and worthwhile from a cost/benefit perspective. Success of a school district requires active and significant awareness and involvement of the non-instructional component of the system in all aspects of the educational delivery process.

Changing Nature of the Administrative Team. In the past, one or two professionals may have been all that comprised a district's non-instructional or business operation staff. When information or input was needed from the business management office, the process was relatively simple—nothing more than interaction between one or two personnel. However, many school districts are staffed much differently today. As a result of the increasing complexity of delivering public education, specialists have emerged. In most modern school systems it has become apparent that no one person can handle the myriad tasks required both to operate effectively and satisfy the growing array of federal, state, and local laws, policies, rules, and regulations in which education functions.

As a result, specialists with specific training and knowledge have emerged in such areas as personnel, communications, legislation, pupil personnel services, transportation, legal services, data processing, foodservice, special education, negotiations, labor relations, facilities management, grants management, risk management, fixed assets management, and cash management. Thus, the concept of "team" also has become crucial to successful operation *within* the business management sector of school districts. Today's school business administrator must not only serve effectively as a member of the superintendent's management team, but must also be able to institute a team concept within his or her own sector of the school district. Such teams must necessarily promote effective communication and coordination among the variety of professionals who directly carry out the school system's specific business and support functions.

Making the task of creating an effective team even more critical today is the fact that many school systems have been forced to reduce and/or consolidate district-level positions. Hence, many school business administrators have had to find creative ways to carry out increasingly complex duties with fewer personnel. By using a coordinated team, whose efforts are mutually supportive and effective, these school business administrators have remained successful despite fewer human resources.

The Service Concept

Successful modern school business administration is not an end in itself. School business management exists for the sole purpose of facilitating the school or school district's educational program. It should operate to support the teacher in the classroom, the principal, and the school board and central administration as each strives to fulfill its responsibilities in accomplishing a mutually identified and agreed upon educational mission.

Today's school business administrator is charged with the responsibility of performing or directing the non-instructional services in a way that best supports the instructional program. In that regard, the effective school business official is one who understands the primary goals of education and who works closely with others in promoting the best education his or her community can afford.

Successful school business administrators imbue their staffs with an understanding of the important role of education in our society and inspire them to have a zeal for service. They help their staffs appreciate how the work of the non-instructional personnel helps to maintain and strengthen effective inter-relationships within the community. The team can contribute much to the continuing community support for education by furnishing its services in a manner perceived by the community and other members of the educational organization to be efficient, economical, and supportive.

Summary

The school business official of the 21st century is a highly trained and respected member of a management team responsible for a nation's most important product—the education of its children. The modern school business official must not only be knowledgeable and skilled in the technical aspects of school district operation, but must also be highly skilled as a communicator and team player. As a key member of a school district's administrative team, today's school business administrator provides critical information and advice to superintendents, school boards, and communities as they chart the educational future of the community's children.

School business managers are no longer envisioned as a green-visored bean counter. Instead, they are recognized as the "chief financial officers" of school systems akin to private-sector professionals who manage the vast resources of multi-national corporations.

ASBO International Professional Registration Program Opportunity Enhanced Professionalism

The ASBO International Professional Registration Program offers both acknowledgement and recognition for professionals on all levels of school business management. Professional registration is a way of identifying the true professionals in the field, the ones with the background, and training and on-the-job experience to merit the honor.

Registration Choices

Professional registration is available at three levels:

- **Registered School Business Administrator (RSBA)**. A professional with overall administrative responsibility for the school system's business functions and who has attained a master's degree.

- **Registered School Business Official (RSBO)** A professional with overall administrative responsibility for one area in the school system's business functions and who holds an undergraduate degree.

- **Registered School Business Specialist (RSBS)**. A professional with administrative responsibility for one area in the school system's business functions who does not hold a college degree.

Benefits of Registration

ASBO International's Professional Registration Program is the highest honor of professional achievement in school business management. It is a mark of distinction. The professional registration designations benefit school business officials in a variety of ways:

- increased credibility in the education community
- use of the registration's initials (RSBA, RSBO, or RSBS) after your name on business stationery, cards, etc.
- better ability to compete in the job market, and
- increased remuneration and benefits on the job.

The ASBO registration program acknowledges the essential principles of adult learning, recognizing a candidate's work experiences and other life accomplishments, particularly those areas in school business administration which are most reflective of successful professional attainment.

Objectives of Registration

ASBO has established the registration program to accomplish four objective. These include:

- To raise the professional standards of those engaged in school business administration.
- To improve the practice of business administration by encouraging school business officials to participate in a continuing program of professional development.
- To identify persons with acceptable knowledge of the principles and practices of school business administration, related disciplines, and laws governing and affecting schools through fulfilling prescribed standards of performance and conduct.
- To award special recognition to school business officials who have demonstrated a high level of competence and ethical fitness for school business administration.

Eligibility

The requirements for consideration for the RSBA, RSBO, or RSBS designation include documented evidence of successful school business administration skills, participation in continuing education programs and demonstrated leadership in the profession and in the community.

Applicants must meet the following prerequisites:

- Be a member of ASBO International for at least 36 consecutive months before January 1 of the year application is made.
- Be employed on a full-time basis in a school business management position for three consecutive years in one school or school system or five years in the school business field.
- Have acceptable character, ability, and reputation confirmed in writing by their school superintendent.
- Pledge to adhere to the ASBO International Code of Ethics and Standards of Conduct.

Meet the education and administrative responsibility requirement(s) of the designation (RSBA, RSBO or RSBS) applied. These requirements were approved by the ASBO International Board of Directors originally in 1964, revised in January 1976 and in January 1979, and effective February 1979.

Additional Requirements for a Registered School Business Administrator

Persons dealing with the total area of school business administration will be designated as School Business Administrators. To be eligible, an applicant must:

- Be that employee member of the school or college staff who has been designated by the board of education and/or the superintendent or college president to have general responsibility for the administration of the business affairs of the employing school system or college. Whatever the administrative organization, the applicant shall be responsible for carrying out the administration of the general business management of the school system or college. Unless otherwise provided by the local law or custom (as in dual control areas), the applicant shall report to the Board of Education through the superintendent of schools, or to the Board of Trustees (or its equivalent) through the college president. To meet this requirement, the school business administrator must have charge of at least three of the categories of responsibility listed and at least 12 specific areas listed on the application form.

- Have earned a minimum of a master's degree from a regionally accredited college or university in an area of school business management, or in educational administration. A photocopy of the degree or an official college transcript of graduate work completed must be received by ASBO before an application can be reviewed. Note: A master's specialist or doctoral degree in a related field may be substituted.

- Have completed a minimum of three years of satisfactorily demonstrated general administrative experience in school business administration, documented in such a way that it can be easily verified.

- Submit an administrative organization chart with his or her official application. This chart must show various administrative and supervisory positions in the school system or college, as adopted by the proper board of education or board of college trustees with the name and complete address of the board of education or college thereon, and the date of the meeting when it was officially adopted and appeared in the minutes. The chart must accurately indicate applicant's position as the top (or equivalent to the top) school business administrator.

Additional Requirements for a Registered School Business Official

Persons dealing with specific areas of school business administration will be referred to as School Business Officials. To be eligible, an applicant must:

- Have overall administrative responsibility for a specific (specialized) area or areas of school business administration in a school system as specified in the application form.

- Have earned a minimum of a bachelor's degree from a regionally accredited college or university. A photocopy of the degree, or a transcript of the work completed, must be received by ASBO before an application can be reviewed.

- Have completed a minimum of three years of satisfactory supervisory or administrative experience, demonstrating competency and ability in effectively supervising personnel and operations in a specific area of school business administration listed in the application form.

- Submit an administrative organization chart with his or her official application. This chart must show the various administrative and supervisory positions in the school system, or college, as adopted by the proper board of education or board of college trustees, with the name and complete address of the board of education or board of college trustees thereon, and the date of the meeting when it was officially adopted and appears in the minutes. The chart must accurately indicate applicant's supervisory position as a school business official in an area of school business operation, and preferably also show the number of personnel the applicant actually supervises.

Additional Requirements for a Registered School Business Specialist

Persons having overall administrative responsibility for a specific (specialized) area or areas of school business administration in a school system will be referred to as a Registered School Business Specialist. To be eligible, an applicant must:

- Have completed a minimum of three (3) years of satisfactory supervisory or administrative experience, demonstrating competency and ability in effectively supervising personnel and operations in a specific area of school business administration listed in K the application form.

- Submit an administrative organization chart with his or her official application. This chart must show the various administrative and supervisory positions in the school system, or college, as adopted by the proper board of education or board of college trustees with the name and complete address of the board of education or board of college trustees thereon and the date of the meeting when it was officially adopted and appears in the minutes. The chart must accurately indicate applicant's supervisory position as a school business official, or specialist in an area of school business operation, and preferably also show the number of personnel the applicant actually supervises.

Maintaining Registration

The continuing education of school business officials is essential to enable schools to cope with rapidly changing conditions. To ensure the highest level of professionalism at all levels of school business management, the Professional Registration Program of ASBO International requires recertification every five years. Mandating recertification ensures that registrants maintain their expertise in the field by participating in continuing education and professional development activities. Maintaining the RSBA, RSBO, or RSBS designation requires the participant to make a concerted effort to continually hone their professional expertise.

To remain registered, a school business official must accumulate professional credits and submit a completed registration renewal form to ASBO International every five years. This form will demonstrate the accumulation of 15 points through participation in various professional development activities and leadership roles.

Registration Renewal

The first renewal date is on the sixth January 1 following the date appearing on the certificate attesting to registration. After initial reregistration, you must continue to renew at five-year intervals (with the renewal reporting form due by the November 1 preceding the registration renewal date). Professional credits for registration renewal can be accumulated anytime from the date appearing on the certificate to the November 1 immediately preceding the next renewal date. For example, officials registered and receiving a certificate dated in 1996 must file a record of 15 professional points earned with the ASBO International Headquarters on or before November 1, 2001 and their registration will be renewed effective January 1, 2002.

Life Registration

An RSBA, RSBO, or RSBS retired from school business and at least age 55 or upon reaching the age of 60, and holding a current registration, is registered for life. No further renewal reporting is necessary.

Fees

A fee is charged for the initial registration and each five-year renewal period. This fee partially offsets the cost of administering the registration program. For more information, contact ASBO.

Chapter 2

The School Business Administrator as Manager

Being an Effective Administrator

As part of the management team, the school business administrator must be a good manager and understand the nature of the basic management functions. Various groups have identified different functions to explain the management process. Fayol's work in 1916 has been credited by Hill (1960) with identifying the original list of management functions. Hill (1960) expanded and applied a similar list to school business administration. McGuffey (1980) identified a similar list of seven functions. Hoy and Miskel (1994) reiterated these as they reviewed theory and research on effective management. This section provides a composite of the functions identified by management theorists and researchers.

Broad Functions of Effective Management

School business administrators have specific responsibilities such as preparing budgets or monitoring the capital construction program. However, certain basic and generic leadership or management tools are needed by all. These include the following:

Planning. From a procedural standpoint, planning should occur before any other management function. Planning involves setting goals, formulating and recommending policy, forecasting and assessing needs, and considering alternative strategies to accomplish the goals. Planning looks ahead and prepares for the future by anticipating opportunities and difficulties, and setting a plan of action to achieve a selected objective or goal.

Strategic planning has become an integral part of setting the direction for school systems. A school business administrator must have a working knowledge of cooperative planning. He or she must also assure that the goals of the business management function are aligned with the overall goals of the system. Further, an effective school business administrator views planning as a tool, rather than an end in and of itself, that permeates the regular activities of the organization. Planning is ongoing. Advancement toward goals must be monitored and action plans adjusted based on continuous feedback and analysis of progress.

Organization. Organization is creating and maintaining all the necessary conditions and relationships to achieve planned objectives or goals. This requires combining the work tasks to be accomplished into appropriate groups, assigning the work to those who are to accomplish it, and delegating the authority necessary to effect its performance. Within this process, proper coordination among individuals and groups must be clearly outlined and lines of authority properly established.

With the decentralization of decision making in many school systems today, organizing to deliver services takes on new meaning. The modern school business administrator must be willing and able to interact with school-based leaders—or communities in many cases—before making final decisions about what will be done by whom and to what standard. Organizing today also requires flexibility to adapt rapidly. In an ever-changing world, tasks not existing yesterday may become the paramount focus of tomorrow. Effective school business administrators view organizing as an ongoing process, never complete, and ever evolving.

Staffing. Staffing means providing competent personnel to accomplish established goals. Staffing implies the ability to screen, select, and employ personnel adequately qualified to fill the positions necessary to meet the needs of the organization. Staffing also involves establishing procedures for replacing and promoting employees, appraising their performance, improving their skills, and developing a compensation system. This process creates new jobs and positions, each requiring a job description and specifications.

Because the team approach is such an integral part of successful school operation today, school business administrators must hire personnel who have good interpersonal skills. Equally important, school business administrators must create a work environment that promotes an open exchange of ideas and rewards staff for creativity and productivity. Finally, staffing must be viewed as ongoing. Job tasks change, resources come and go. Effective school business administrators are constantly reviewing staff allocations and assignments and adjusting these as changing priorities dictate.

Influencing or Directing. To accomplish the organization's objectives, employees must be motivated to achieve the objectives assigned to their positions. This management function has numerous dimensions including morale, employee satisfaction, employee productivity, communications, and leadership. It involves directing people and procedures. Its purpose is getting things done with a maximum of self-realization and effective participation by the staff.

In the school district of the 21st century, this means recognizing the value of shared decision making. It also means learning that effective leadership does not necessarily mean exertion of absolute control. In the modern school system, the school business administrator is a facilitator, not a dictator. Effective school business administrators use shared decision making, decentralized decision making, and multiple sources of input whenever possible to gain needed insight and perspective on an issue.

Controlling. Controlling is regulating action in relation to a plan. The controlling function is the process that measures performance against standards and ensures that errors are corrected so that work is accomplished according to expectations. It assumes that those responsible for management can anticipate potential sources of deviation from performance standards and seek means of correction before occurrence, rather than after. Three basic activities are necessary in establishing an effective control procedure: standards must be set and understood, performance must be checked against standards, and a procedure must be developed to activate corrective action when necessary.

Controlling or regulating to meet performance standards is not a top-down process. Employees should not only be involved actively in setting goals and standards, but also in monitoring quality of output and in providing significant input to improve district operations. Whether it is referred to as Total Quality Management or Shared Decision Making, staff involvement in "controlling" outcomes is a major tool in achieving organizational goals in the twenty-first century.

Coordination. Coordination is obtaining the proper relationships among the people involved in a task or activity. It refers not only to activities directly under a specific manager's control, but also to relationships and communication with activities outside the manager's immediate control. For example, school administrators must frequently work with community agencies over which they have no control.

Today, coordination is one of the most critical roles of successful management, particularly for school business administrators. Because everything is so complex and changes rapidly, finding the right mix of people and resources has become a major challenge. Compounding this is the growing realization that a single model or approach will not work in all situations. Each situation is unique, requiring the school business administrator to constantly develop, redevelop, and coordinate ad hoc teams/resources to accomplish tasks. The effective school business administrator realizes that success often is affected by outside entities and includes these in planning and decision making.

Decision Making. Decision making is selecting a choice from among competing alternatives: conscious deliberations by a manager about the alternative ways to use available resources. It is a conscious effort at discrimination among alternative actions. Decision making is basic to every function of management and is involved in all management functions. It should be a deliberate process, wherever possible, in which the consequences of available alternatives are carefully weighed before a choice is made.

However, in modern society, decision making mirrors the increasing complexity of the world. As a result, effective decision making has taken on new meaning. Instead of being something done exclusively by the manager, it is shared with the team involved in carrying out the resulting decision. Further, intuitive decision making has emerged as a legitimate form of choosing among complex options. This approach to decision making is sometimes referred to as doing "what feels right" or going with the "gut" or "heart." Intuitive decision-making recognizes that the intricacies of some problems or situations do not lend themselves either to having complete data or time for contemplation that the traditional rational decision-making model requires. However, for intuitive decision making to be successful, those using it must possess two qualifications: knowledge and experience in school business management.

Evaluation. Evaluation is the process of determining the extent to which organizational goals and objectives are being met. It is a continuous process of determining whether or not the courses of action being taken and the performance results achieved are fulfilling the mission and goals of an organization. Every function of an organization, its management activities, and ongoing work events should be under continuous appraisal. Both internal and external audits should be used to evaluate the organization's performance.

Critical to the evaluation process today is recognition that school systems now operate in a highly pluralistic, changing culture. As a result, there are diverse and often competing expectations for schools and for the organizational components supporting those schools. Effective managers, as part of the evaluation process, constantly scan or monitor their environments for signs of changing expectations and goals. Similarly, such administrators actively involve their various constituents in establishing organizational goals, monitoring outcomes, and periodically assessing the overall effectiveness and efficiency of the administrator's organizational responsibilities.

Communicating. Communicating is the act of *effectively* sending *and* receiving information. Modern researchers of effective business practice indicate that communications is one of the most important determinants of a leader's success. Effective communication involves not only establishing formal channels of interaction, but also creating an environment where employees feel that the work setting is open and non-threatening enough to provide honest, meaningful input.

Successful school business administrators actively seek to communicate not only with employees, but also with other sectors of the organization and the community. They encourage the exchange of information, points of view, and philosophical positions that might affect the operation of the business management function.

The Specific Tasks of School Business Administration

While there are generic management tools and tasks that a school business administrator should use, these must be applied to specific job functions or responsibilities. The specific duties and job tasks of the school business official can be grouped or clustered into several categories.

Tasks delineate the work areas of school business administration. They are best identified through broad task clusters that represent the work areas associated with school business administration. Numerous writers have identified work areas or task clusters in school business administration[1]. In 1980, McGuffey identified 28 task clusters—one general and 27 specific areas—after examining the work of more than 20 authors. He validated these 28 clusters through a random national sample of school business administrators. Since 1980 these clusters or distinct job responsibilities have been regularly reaffirmed[2]. Specific work/task clusters most often identified with school business management include:

- Capital Fund Management
- Cash Management
- Classified Personnel Management
- Community Relations
- Construction Management
- Data Processing
- Educational Facilities Planning
- Educational Resource Management

- Financial Planning and Budgeting
- Fiscal Accounting and Financial Reporting
- Fiscal Audits and Reports
- Food Services
- Grantsmanship
- Insurance and Risk Management
- Legal Control
- Office Management
- Payroll Management
- Plant Maintenance
- Plant Operations
- Plant Security and Property Protection
- Professional Negotiations
- Property Management
- Purchasing
- Staff Development
- Student Activity Funds
- Transportation Services
- Warehousing and Supplies Management

These clusters encompass many of the specific tasks performed by practicing school business officials and school business administrators. They are also a careful delineation of related task activities frequently used as the basis for subdividing school business administrators' work and establishing school business officials' responsibilities and authority limits.

It should be noted that these clusters do not specifically include the broad spectrum of responsibilities for assessing, levying, and collecting taxes required in many districts. Nor are such tasks as elections, bond and tax referenda, minute book and public records management, property custody functions, or other similar duties included. However, by law in some states and provinces, the Board Secretary must or may be the School Business Administrator and Board Secretary or District Clerk simultaneously, and, thus, hold these and other responsibilities as well.

Emerging, New Responsibilities

Two additional job tasks critical to successful school business management have emerged in the past several years. These are effectively interacting with the media and constructively interfacing with local, state, and national legislative/policy bodies.

Media Task. Education often is the biggest business in a community. It is supported by substantial amounts of tax dollars. As a result, education has become increasingly newsworthy. School business officials must be prepared to interact effectively with various print and audio/visual media. This means building positive working relations with the press and newscasters, developing a media interaction plan, and providing honest, clear, and informative responses when approached by the media.

Political Task. Various agencies at the local, state, and national levels are competing for limited public resources. Similarly, in an increasingly pluralistic society, special interest groups exert as much influence as they can to promote their agendas—agendas that are not always in the best interests of public education. Today's school business administrator must become more politically involved than ever before. This includes such activities as:

- developing or supporting legislative agendas,
- building close working relationships with elected officials and agency decision makers, and
- monitoring and reacting to legislative and policy proposals arising from various local, state, and national elected bodies.

Summary

The job of school business administrator is both complex and challenging. Job tasks are diverse and highly technical and emerging tasks, such as effectively interacting with the media and involvement in the "politics" of education, make the job even more demanding. The modern school business administrator must be a highly skilled individual with exceptional communication and human relations skills.

[1] *Linn, 1956; Knezevich and Fowlkes, 1960; Hill, 1960, 1970; Jordan, 1969; Kaiser and Webb, 1974; McGuffey, 1980; Wood, 1995; Everett, 1996*
[2] *Tharpe, 1995*

Chapter
3

The Broad Responsibilities of the School Business Administrator

Authority to do the Job

As a member of the superintendent's cabinet, the school business administrator is a part of the team that helps to develop, recommend, and thus, determine school policy. Therefore, it is important that this officer's responsibilities are well defined and that he or she be given the authority to act. Authority is vital to allowing the school business administrator to be uninhibited in discharging assigned responsibilities within the framework of the established policies of the district. Appropriate delegation also relieves the superintendent from worry about the daily functions of school business management. The superintendent should be able to depend upon the professional school business administrator to provide information and services to increase the entire organization's effectiveness in public education.

Ensuring adequate representation of the business function on the superintendent's leadership team—whether by one person or several—is essential. This team develops and recommends policies and procedures dealing with the total educational program. Today it is clearly understood that most educational decisions have financial and operational consequences. Similarly, most dollar decisions have educational consequences. Therefore, it is critical that the school business area is properly represented when such decisions are being made.

All in a Day's Work of the School Business Administrator

With the foregoing concepts as background, major areas of responsibility for the typical school business administrator may be described. While the many "typical" tasks of the "typical" school business administrator have been carefully catalogued and documented, it is important to keep in mind that the uniqueness of the setting in which a school business administrator works may cause substantial variation from the norm. Such factors as number of personnel, available resources, employee expertise, organizational structure, and even politics can have an impact on what specific responsibilities and authority a particular school business administrator assumes. A "typical" job description of a school business administrator is provided at the end of this chapter that depicts one district's expectations for this important position. Presented below are typical broad job responsibilities associated with school business management.

Financial Planning and Budgeting

This work/task area involves preparing the educational budget, the reconciliating available resources and expected revenues with the fiscal needs of the school or school district, developing and operating a fiscal control system, and implementing and monitoring long-term fiscal planning in the context of community resources and needs. The school business administrator must be aware of and sensitive to changes in the community's economic base and alert to all sources of revenue and outside events affecting the community. This mandates that the school business administrator be well versed on taxation at all levels and recognize that the system is constantly dealing with scarce resources. The school business administrator employs strategic planning, systems analysis, and such concepts of planning-programming-budgeting-evaluating systems to all aspects of financial planning to provide the district with the best educational experience for each dollar spent or resource used.

Purchasing

This work/task area provides for the procurement of supply and equipment needs of the school or school district, including the preparation of supply and equipment bids and specifications, and the authorization of payment of supply and equipment invoices. In operating this function, the school business officer often is responsible for all purchases, including equipment and supplies for ongoing programs, and for new buildings as well as for existing ones. The school business administrator must consider the educational implications associated with each purchasing decision, prepare suitable specifications and standards, and use good purchasing principles and procedures. Within this context the school business officer is also often responsible for warehousing, storing, trucking, and inventory control.

       In some instances as a result of decentralization, the school business official becomes more of a facilitator and mentor in the area of purchasing. Particularly with site-based management, at least some purchasing functions have been assigned to principals, changing the school business administrator's role to oversight and coordination.

Warehousing

The responsibilities involved in this work/task area include developing a storage and retrieval plan; implementing the warehousing program; recruiting, selecting and assigning personnel to jobs in the program; establishing a stock locator system; coordinating and monitoring the stock receiving, storage, and distribution system; and conducting a periodic internal audit of the warehouse stock. Other responsibilities include the development of an appropriate warehouse inventory system, the arrangement of physical stock in the warehouse proper, the preparation of a warehouse catalog, and the continuous appraisal of the warehousing program. In many school systems, this task service area also involves selling surplus items and conducting all salvage and disposal programs as authorized by the district.

Facilities

Facilities Planning and Construction. In this area, the school business manager works with administrators, teachers, and lay personnel, as well as regulatory officials, in determining and planning for school plant needs and acquiring school sites. Responsibility also includes development of educational and technical standards for new and renovated structures. Other duties entail working with architects to see that needs are properly translated into final plans, interacting with attorneys and financial advisors to effect suitable financing, working with bidders to secure economical contracts, and interacting with contractors and construction management providers to secure quality construction at reasonable costs.

Within the facilities category , the school business administrator often oversees the district's school plant needs and its short and long range plans to meet those needs. Other duties include preparing educational specifications, coordinating and monitoring facilities construction, and providing a system for the continuous appraisal of the educational facilities planning program. Other critical roles in this area are

- designing and implementing a system to prioritize projects — especially when funding is limited,
- determining if a structure can be effectively and efficiently renovated or must be replaced, and

- working with the community and school board to secure sufficient funding to meet the facilities needs of the district.

Facilities Mothballing, Disposal, Conversion, Remodeling/Modernizing. In this task area, the school business administrator assists the chief school officer and school board in evaluating the educational utility of existing school plants and in establishing an order of priority for the disposal, conversion, remodeling/modernizing, or mothballing of facilities. The school business officer works with educational program experts and community agencies in determining the long-term potential need for particular school buildings and facilities. He or she also works with the maintenance and operations staffs, as well as architects and engineers, in determining the comparative costs of utilizing different facilities and/or the relative merits of modernizing one facility versus another.

The potential impacts of curriculum reorganization or modification of instructional delivery systems, different academic organizational formats, modification of school district boundaries, and future community demographic and economic trends must all be evaluated. Eventually an acceptable set of criteria for the de-selection or continuation of school facilities must be established.

If it is determined that a particular school facility is to be taken out of service, the school business administrator then frequently works with other community agencies in deciding how that school plant is to be disposed of. In recent years, school plants have been converted into municipal government facilities, such as town and village halls; senior citizens housing complexes; libraries; low rent housing projects or other neighborhood agency and program centers. In addition, some have been sold for private development into garden apartments, loft storage buildings, churches, office and professional centers, stores and for many other uses, including private and parochial schools.

Many districts have also converted surplus school buildings into school administration and office centers, maintenance shops, storage warehouses, adult and youth program centers, senior citizen centers, and specialized training facilities for federal and state programs. In some cases, these buildings have been used as daycare nurseries, and as general community recreational and activity centers. In still other cases, where future pupil population trends and school housing needs are difficult to predict or are subject to volatile community economic and employment trends, school facilities have been kept on a "mothballed" or standby status.

School Plant Maintenance and Care. This work task area involves preparing a comprehensive plan to manage plant maintenance, implementation of the program, recruitment and assignment of personnel and staff organization, coordination of work activities, and continuous appraisal of the program. Included are responsibilities for keeping school plants and other functions operating effectively through a combination of general and preventative maintenance. Keeping structures clean, healthful, and safe also fall under this job task.

Plant Security and Property Protection. This task area includes planning and developing a comprehensive program of property protection including plant security, safety, and fire protection. This includes organizing the program; recruiting, selecting, and assigning personnel to jobs; coordinating and monitoring the program; developing a management control system and the continuous appraisal of the property protection program.

Community Use of School Facilities. The school business officer, working with the plant operations personnel, instructional staff, community leaders, and lay citizens, plays a key role in developing policies and procedures for community use of school facilities. The lighted schoolhouse is an important manifestation of good community relations. Citizens now expect their expensive school plants to serve a variety of school and community activities. Developing reasonable and adequate usage regulations, establishing fee schedules, implementing a permit approval process, and developing a calendar scheduling process are important facets of this function.

School Community Relations

The responsibilities in this work/task area include developing and implementing a community relations plan involving school business affairs; providing appropriate information to the chief school officer and the school board regarding the business operations of the school district; communicating accomplishments, needs, and services of the school business operations to the community; using various media to provide public understanding of school business affairs; and the continuous appraisal of community response and feedback on the school business program. It also includes developing effective links with schools, particularly as decentralization occurs.

Working in this area, the school business officer helps explain the educational program to the public by preparing informational materials for distribution; working with service clubs, the PTA and citizens' committees; and establishing contacts with press, radio, and television services; providing the superintendent, other staff members, and the school board with facts that can help them in their relations with the public; and interpreting the business area of educational programs to the public and to the educational staff.

Personnel Management

The responsibilities in this job area include recruiting or helping to secure personnel for all school business management positions; handling individual and group problems related to working conditions, benefits, policies and procedures; and providing guidance and information to terminated personnel.

Non-Instructional Personnel Management. The responsibilities of this work/task area include developing a management plan, recruiting and assigning personnel, preparing job descriptions, appraising workloads, maintaining a personnel records system for non-instructional personnel, and continually monitoring and appraising the non-instructional personnel program. Other responsibilities include developing an orientation program for new personnel, formulating a wage and salary plan, evaluating the performance of non-instructional personnel, and developing a program for producing agreements on working conditions, salaries, wages, and benefits between the school district and non-instructional personnel.

In-Service Training for Non-Instructional Staff Development. This work/task area includes responsibility for determining the staff development needs among the administrative personnel, preparing and implementing a staff development program, and providing for the continuous program appraisal. Specific responsibilities in this area include: organizing and directing a program of in-service training aimed at increasing the skills of school business management personnel and at developing proper attitudes toward the educational objectives of the school district. Involvement of staff in determining their professional needs can significantly enhance the effectiveness of employee training and development programs.

Collective Negotiations. The responsibilities of this work/task area include preparing plans for collective negotiations of various employee groups, developing negotiating strategies, analyzing and evaluating employee proposals, and directing the negotiation process. Other responsibilities involve interpreting negotiated contracts to management personnel and the continuous appraisal of policies, practices, and procedures used by management in the negotiation process.

Employee Benefits Programs. It is generally the responsibility of the school business officer to oversee the administration and operation of various employee benefit programs. Pension and retirement contributions and deductions, health and hospital insurance, dental insurance, sick leave, personal leave, sabbatical leave payments, vacation allowances, cumulative sick leave, and similar benefits are frequently operated as auxiliary records of the payroll operations. The majority of districts require the school business officer to make periodic reports to employees on the status of their benefits, and many districts present updated accumulation totals on various withholdings, contributions, voluntary deductions for community funds, government bond purchases, voluntary credit union withholdings, cumulative sick leave, and cumulative vacation credits on periodic payroll reports or regular paycheck stubs. The volume of records connected with these benefit plans is an emerging and constantly increasing task for the business operation of school districts. Adding to the complexity is the fact that many districts offer employees a wide array of benefits choices. As a result keeping employees informed of current benefits and maintaining accurate records of benefits selected by individual employees are both demanding.

Payroll Management. The responsibilities of this work task area include developing salary schedules; verifying employee services; preparing checks or warrants used in salary payments; authorizing the release of salary payments; funding payroll accounts; preparing special reports required for income tax, social security and retirement, and numerous special withholdings; and the continuous appraisal of the payroll management program.

Fiscal Accounting and Financial Reporting

This work/task area provides for establishing procedures for classifying fund and receipt accounts, managing the fiscal accounting systems including budgetary controls and current operations reports, preparing financial reports and submitting them to the local school board and state board, coordinating and monitoring fiscal accounts, and the continuous appraisal of the accounting system. A specific responsibility is the establishment and supervision of the accounting system necessary to provide school officials and administrators with accurate financial facts as the basis for formulating policies and decisions. Other specific responsibilities include providing the proper safeguards for the custody of public funds and making complete and revealing reports both locally and statewide.

Cash Management. This work/task area involves planning for the management of temporarily idle school funds, preparing a cash investment program, monitoring invested funds. School business officials are involved with reporting investment activities to the school board, and continuously appraising the investment program.

Fiscal Audits and Reports. This work/task area addresses developing a plan for the continuous internal audit of fiscal records to assure the following: regularity and accuracy of fiscal records; pre-audits to prevent unauthorized or illegal expenditures; the systematic investigation, verification, and critical review of financial operations by an independent auditor; regular reports of fiscal effectiveness to the chief school offices and school board; and the continuous appraisal of the fiscal operations of the school district.

Insurance and Risk Management. The responsibilities of this work/task area involve preparing a plan to meet the insurance needs of the school district. This includes determining the coverages needed, establishing the insurable values of buildings and their contents, determining procedures for procuring insurance coverage, reporting losses and filing claims, maintaining appropriate records, and continuously appraising the adequacy of the program.

Capital Fund Management. Activities in the capital fund management work/task area involve determining fiscal costs for the building program of the school district and short- and long-range planning for financing capital improvements. Other tasks include determining methods of financing capital needs, preparing the capital fund budget, making debt service payments, recommending funding options to the superintendent and school board, and accounting for school bond payments and debt service revenues and expenditures.

School Property Management. This work/task area includes developing a comprehensive plan for a property management program, organizing the program and continuously evaluating the program's effectiveness. Specific responsibilities include developing a property accounting system, maintaining an up-to-date inventory of district property, coordinating and monitoring the use of school property, recommending purchase or sale of property as appropriate, and making periodic reports on the status of property owned and used by the school district.

School Activity Funds. The responsibilities of this work/task area include preparing a district-wide plan for the management of school activity or student body funds; recommending policies, rules, and regulations regarding the management of school activity funds; and continuously evaluating the program management. Other responsibilities include the internal audit of school activity funds, establishing appropriate records and reports, and preparing an accounting manual to guide the management of school activity funds. As decentralization and site-based management dictate, duties also may include assisting schools with student and activity fund accounting.

The work also includes similar procedures for school-based internal funds, which are legally required to be handled as funds of the district, such as library fines, laboratory and locker fees, instrument or equipment rentals, and sale of rings, annuals, and other items.

Grantsmanship

The responsibilities in this area include preparing an annual plan for seeking and obtaining grant funds, identifying grant/funding sources, making contact with public agencies and private foundations to obtain grants, preparing and assisting with the preparation of grant proposals and applications, providing fiscal data needed for grant applications, performing the accounting functions relative to grant funds, and submitting fiscal reports to funding agencies or foundations.

To accomplish these tasks, the school business officer assists in obtaining special educational funds from private foundations, state or provincial departments of education, state or provincial legislatures, and federal sources; makes certain that proposals are sound from a business point of view; insures that records are maintained and financial reports published; and requires termination audits of funds and services as evidence of good stewardship.

A relatively new part of this responsibility is assisting various school and school-related components to establish nonprofit foundations. Many schools and school districts have discovered that setting up foundations opens a whole new source of revenue opportunities.

Data Processing

The responsibilities in this work/task area are to determine the data processing needs of the business operation of the school system; develop a plan for collecting, maintaining, and retrieving this information; recruit, assign and organize personnel to perform jobs in data processing; continuously appraise the program; and assure that proper technology is available and used to efficiently process data throughout the system.

To achieve these results, the school business officer uses modern data processing practices to provide better and more complete accounting records. He or she also establishes or assists in establishing appropriate data banks, electronic files, and technological data processing procedures that provide management information for appropriate decision making, forecasting, and evaluation for all subcomponents of the school district, including schools.

The data processing function is broadly defined to include non-business information of all school operations, as well as financial and operational data. Student scheduling, grade reporting, pupil personnel records, census and attendance data, personnel and educational materials, resource files, instructional equipment and supply distribution procedures, student testing, teacher and class profiles, instructional research, and many other applications of data processing are included in the data processing function of a school district. Most of this will be handled through use of computers and related support technology. Security of information, control of access to data, and maintaining back-up files and systems are critical to the modern data processing function.

Technology

A relatively new and extremely important job task of the school business administrator is developing and/or assisting in the development of a technology plan for the school district. This entails not only technology for the traditional data processing processes described above, but technology for instruction. Included are such tasks as determining the role of computers in instruction, how such instruction will be delivered, what equipment will be used, how systems will be maintained, and evaluating the effectiveness of various technological initiatives. Other technological tasks include developing and maintaining distance education systems, including both television and other mediums such as the Internet. A major task today is establishing a maintenance system with sufficient personnel to keep technology working. Equally important, the school business administrator must have a system in place to update and replace equipment and software to stay current.

Legal Control

This work/task area involves a number of activities related to the law and regulation of school business matters and may include preparing employment contracts for personnel; managing vendors' contracts; assisting with the selection of an attorney for the school district; preparing rules, procedures and regulations pertaining to school business affairs; participating in the resolution of legal problems pertaining to the sale and acquisition of school properties; participating in opening bids and awarding contracts; evaluating school board resolutions; publishing official notices and reports; advertising for goods and services; and making a continuing assessment of the potential legal exposure of school board members and school personnel to liability and litigation.

School Transportation Services

Responsibilities in this task area include continuous planning of the transportation program; program organization; recruiting, selecting, and assigning personnel to jobs in the program; and evaluating the program. Specific responsibilities entail developing and implementing a transportation safety program; providing adequate bus repair facilities; developing and continuously monitoring a bus routing plan; recruiting drivers; conducting a driver training program; organizing and operating adequate bus maintenance repair, spare parts, and supply service; maintaining fuel and vandalism security programs; and dealing with personnel issues.

In some districts, the officer in charge of this service works closely with the census and attendance function to establish eligibility zones for transportation at various grade levels, adjudicate demands for transportation services, issue bus passes, and enforce disciplinary codes for student behavior on buses.

Today the school business administrator must also assess the pros and cons of privatizing the transportation function. Even when district chooses private transportation, the school business officer still has a major responsibility in this area. He or she must establish specifications for potential contractors; secure legal bids; supervise the contract operation; administer claims, payments, and penalties; and periodically evaluate the quality and cost effectiveness of the contracted approach.

Legislation and Politics

A growing area of responsibility of the school business administrator is keeping the school system informed of local, state, and national legislative and political activities that may affect the operation of the school district. Responsibilities are varied and include everything from developing draft policies and pieces of legislation, to monitoring legislative sessions of policy-making entities, to establishing a network of contacts that provides information.

School Food Services

This work/task area involves responsibilities for the development of a comprehensive plan for operating the school foodservice program, including recruiting, selecting, and assigning school foodservice personnel; budget preparation; establishing the price of school lunches served; and coordinating the appraisal of the foodservice program. Other responsibilities include internal audits of school foodservice accounts and the planning and provision of the physical arrangements of foodservice programs.

Some specific functions include purchasing food supplies and equipment; preparing specifications and administering major contracts with dairy, bakery, and other vendors; operating food preparation facilities (satellite and central kitchens); and establishing/overseeing refrigeration, trucking, and distribution systems. This work/task area usually involves establishing eligibility procedures for free or reduced cost meals; administering federal and state grants reporting and accounting procedures; and, in some districts, may also involve preschool breakfast and community adult feeding programs. Another major responsibility is hiring, training, and evaluating foodservice personnel. Whether administered by either district personnel or by contract vendors, the foodservice program is part of the overall nutrition and health education programs of the district.

Many districts now contract out the foodservice function. A responsibility of today's school business administrator is to assess the various means of providing foodservice for the school system and recommend to the school board and superintendent the approach that is most cost effective and efficient. This requires not only evaluating financial factors but also such issues as quality control and community and employee perspectives and support.

Summary

As the delineation of the school business administrator's responsibilities provided above suggests, the role is critical to any school system. Clearly, today's school business administrator plays an integral part in almost every aspect of school district operation. More than ever the non-instructional dimensions of school systems play a critical role in the success of the instructional function. A school district today must have a school business administrator with a breadth and depth of understanding of not only the classic business functions such as accounting and budgeting but of the whole school district, including the role of the business function in achieving the school district's instructional goals.

Sample Job Description I

Associate Superintendent for
Business and Financial Services

Department: Business and Financial Services

Requirements:

A. Educational Level: 6-year degree (or equivalent)

B. Certification: Nebraska Professional
                          Administrative and Supervisory
                          Certificate with an Endorsement in the
                          Superintendency

C. Experience Desired: 5 years in General School Administration

D. Other Requirements: General knowledge of Federal and State Statutes as
                          they relate to the Business and Fiscal operations of a
                          school district.

Reports to: The Superintendent of Schools

Receives Guidance
From: The Superintendent of Schools

Essential Functions:

Financial Operations

The specific responsibilities of the Associate Superintendent in the area of
financial operations are as follows:

1. Prepares annual budgets under the direction of the Superintendent and
   Board of Education with the cooperation of the principals and other
   designated staff members, with the budget to be consistent with the educational objectives and financial resources of the school district.

2. Employs sound accounting practices to assure adequate records revealingly
   the administration budget.

3. Serves as the central purchasing agent and carries out all necessary functions of this operation according to adopted budget, policies of the district, laws of the state, and auditing guidelines.

4. Services as director of central district supply and warehouse.

    - Plans and directs the standardization program for equipment and supplies accounting.

    - Plans and directs the warehousing program for equipment and supplies.

    - Plans and directs the inventory and stock control program for equipment and supplies

    - Directs the provision of equipment and supplies to new and existing facilities of the district.

    - Develops policy and recommends budget for an orderly replacement of existing movable equipment as it becomes obsolete.

    - Establishes procedures for estimating the costs for equipping new schools or additions.

5. Supplies and maintains monthly budget balances and financial reports to the Superintendent and the Board of Education at each regular board meeting.

6. Prepares listing of claims for approval by the Board of Education.

7. Requires a regular requisition procedure from all employees properly channeled through principals, classified directors, and other staff members in sufficient time for cost-effective purchase of supplies in quantities through competitive bidding.

8. Signs purchase orders as authorized by the Board of Education.

9. Supervises and evaluates classified personnel responsible for accounting, purchasing, and other clerical work.

10. Maintains written manuals of procedures for budget development, requisitions, purchasing and payments.

11. Prepares financial records for the annual audit as required by the laws of the state.

12. Invests all receipts and cash reserves according tot he investment laws of the state and the cashflow needs of the district.

13. Provides for staff development of all employees involved in the financial operations of the district.

14. Monitors all funds for proper accounting and approval of expenditures for

all funds.

15. Reports to Superintendent and Board of Education on the annual audit.

16. Works with the Building/Finance Committee of the Board of Education in bidding and budget preparation.

17. Develops and directs bidding process and procedures for purchasing.

Maintenance of District Properties

The specific responsibilities of the Associate Superintendent in maintaining district properties are as follows:

1. Supervises and evaluates the performance of the Supervisor of Buildings and Grounds.

2. Supervises all operations and maintenance work.

3. Initiates, supervises, and evaluates all major maintenance, building, and remodeling work.

4. Ensures that buildings, grounds and ancillary equipment are maintained in safe, sanitary condition, and coordinates safety programs in buildings and grounds.

5. Checks buildings, grounds, and ancillary equipment for safety in compliance with fire department and state officials.

6. Ensures compliance's of buildings and grounds with local, state and federal codes.

7. Ensures that all maintenance vehicles and fleet vehicles are properly cared for, maintained, and scheduled.

8. Provides for staff development of maintenance employees.

Marketing and Economic Development

The specific responsibilities of the Associate Superintendent's role with custodians are as follows:

1. Seeks ways to increase availability and access to markets through local businesses, agents, and agencies.

2. Seeks ways to market school programs and services throughout private and public community.

3. Seeks ways to work cooperatively with other public agencies to share programs, services and personnel whenever possible and cost-effective.

Supervision of Custodial Staff

The specific responsibilities of the Associate Superintendent's role with custodians are as follows:

1. Actively works with the Supervisor of Buildings and Grounds in the recruitment of custodians and maintenance workers.
2. Provides for evaluation of all custodians.
3. Actively works with the Supervisor of Buildings and Grounds in the assignment of custodial personnel to each building.
4. Approves the overtime for all service personnel.
5. Provides for staff development of custodians.

School Lunch Program

1. Supervises and evaluates performance of the Director of Food Services.
2. Provides for evaluation of all food service personnel.
3. Works directly with the Director of Food Services in budgeting, purchasing, commodities, equipment and supplies.
4. Reports monthly to the Superintendent and the Board of Education on purchases and accounting for the lunch program.
5. Provides for the staff development of food service employees.

Other Responsibilities

The specific responsibilities of the Associate Superintendent's role in other areas are as follows:

1. Provides for inventories of all equipment in the district.
2. Develops insurance programs to cover liability for property and actions.
3. Provides for rental of school facilities by community groups.
4. Provides for a school census of all children age 0 to 21 as required by state law.
5. Assumes other responsibilities as assigned by the Superintendent.
6. Performs the duties of the Superintendent when the Superintendent and Assistant Superintendent are absent from the district.
7. Monitors and reviews state and federal legislation advising the Superintendent on matters affecting the district.

Annual Performance Plan

The specific responsibilities of the Associate Superintendent in the annual performance plan.

1. Develops and implements annual performance plan.
2. Reviews job descriptions.
3. Sets annual performance goals and submits self-assessment of performance.

Board Secretary

The specific responsibilities of the Associate Superintendent as Board Secretary are as follows:

1. Gives public notice and attends all meetings of the Board.
2. Keeps full and accurate minutes of all meetings of the Board and sends a copy of such minutes to each member of the Board at least one week prior to the next regular meeting of the Board.
3. Assists in the preparation of agendas setting forth all known items of business to be considered at the Board meeting.
4. Publishes all legal notices concerning District business.
5. Performs other such tasks as may be from time to time assigned.

District Treasurer

The specific responsibilities of the Associate Superintendent as District Treasurer are as follows:

1. Acts as custodian of all money belonging to the District.
2. Receives all monies belonging to the District.
3. Deposits monies received in banks designated by the Board.
4. Gives a bond in such sum as shall be required before entering the duties of the office, the premium on such bond to be paid by the Board.
5. Pays out District's monies on written order of designated officials of the Board.
6. Gives detailed accounts of money received and disbursed at least once a month prior to the regular meeting of the Board.
7. Prepares and submits a monthly report of the Districts fiscal status.
8. Renders a full annual report at the end of each fiscal year.

Negotiator

The specific responsibilities of the Associate Superintendent as Negotiator are as follows:

1. Negotiates with certified bargaining unit to arrive at a mutually satisfactory agreement on salaries, hours, and working conditions of employees represented by the bargaining unit.
2. Selects appropriate management personnel for the negotiating team.
3. Directs the accumulation of necessary data used in negotiations, such as salaries and fringe benefits comparisons and comparative contract language.
4. Recommends agreements to the Finance Committee for approval.
5. Discusses requests from non-certified groups on wages, hours, and working conditions, and makes recommendation concerning these discussions to the Superintendent and Director of Personnel.
6. Acts as official designate of the superintendent at appropriate staves of the grievance procedure.
7. Plans, organizes, and represents the District in fact findings and representation cases heard before the Commission of Industrial Relations.
8. Coordinates all aspects of contract administration during term of various contracts with employee organizations.
9. Interprets the negotiated agreement to members of the staff, as appropriate.

Computer Systems Administration

1. Serves as the Systems Administrator in the operation of the HP3000 computer system.
   - Monitors and controls access to non-sharable peripherals.
   - Initiates, monitors, and controls jobs and sessions.
   - Monitors and controls printing activity.
   - Schedules and performs full and partial systems backups and recovers files from backup tapes.
   - Shuts down and starts up the system hardware and operating system when appropriate.

- Adds terminals to the system configuration when needed.
- Monitors the systems log files and manages the systems free space.
- Troubleshoots problems with terminals, tapedrives and printers.
- Identifies problems and performs recovery operations from system interruptions.
- Performs a memory sysdump when appropriate.
- Develops and maintains a standard operating procedures manual for the HP3000 system.

Physical Requirements

		Never	Occasional	Frequent	Constant
A.	Standing		X		
B.	Walking		X		
C.	Sitting				X
D.	Bending/ Stooping	X			
E.	Reaching/ Pushing/ Pulling	X			
F.	Climbing	X			
G.	Driving	X			
H.	Lifting 20# Max		X		
I.	Carrying 25 ft.		X		
J.	Manual Dexterity Tasks:			X	

Specify: Telephone
Typewriter/Word Processor
Dictaphone
Computer
Microfiche reader

Other Requirements (Intellectual, Sensory):
Skills in oral and written communication
Skills in math and logical thinking
Effective leadership capabilities

Working Conditions:

A.   Inside X   Outside   Both

B.   Climatic Environment:
Primary work area is air conditioned.

C.   Hazards:

Sample Job Description II

Business Manager

Qualifications:

1. High School Diploma with five years financial and business manager experience OR College degree in Business and Accounting preferably two years experience.
2. Ability to maintain financial records and fiscal accountability.
3. Ability to communicate effectively with staff and community in all written and oral communications.
4. Ability to utilize and operate computers and software.
5. Ability to manage time effectively.
6. Ability to maintain confidentiality at all times.
7. Such alternatives to the above qualifications as the Board may find appropriate and acceptable.

Reports to: Superintendent of Schools

Supervises: Administrative Office Staff and Building Secretarial Staff

Job Goal: To administer the business affairs of the District in such a way as to provide the best possible educational services with the financial resources available.

Performance Responsibilities:

1. Supervise the management of the financial affairs of the schools.
2. Assist the Superintendent with the budget development and long-range financial planning.
3. Establish and supervise a program of accounting adequate to record in detail all money and credit transactions.
4. Supervise all accounting operations.
5. Manage the District's investment of idle funds. (If there is another person as Treasurer, to work with the Treasurer in the investment of District funds).
6. Act as payroll officer for the District.

7. Supervise the collection , safekeeping and distribution of all funds.

8. Manage the District's insurance programs for both employees and property.

9. Assign duties to and supervise the work of the administrative office clerical staff.

10. Act as advisor to the superintendent on all questions relating to the business and financial affairs of the District.

11. Assist in recruiting, hiring, training, supervising, and evaluating all clerical and financial personnel.

12. Arrange for the internal auditing of school accounts.

13. Approve vouchers and invoices.

14. Conduct cost analysis, financial, salary and wage, and fringe benefits surveys.

15. Obtain comparative prices and quotations for purchase and delivery of goods and services.

16. Determine employees' placement on appropriate wage scales.

17. Manage all personnel records, including personnel files, teacher certificates, approval statements, sick leave, time cards, etc.

18. Distribute wage and tax statements to employees and files wage and tax statements with government agencies.

19. Maintain petty cash.

20. Management District's tax-sheltered annuity program.

21. Work closely and cooperatively with independent auditors. Notify the Auditor of the State of the independent auditors contracted and supply copies of the audit to the State Auditor and Department of Education. Notify local media of completed audits, and have the audit report available for the public.

22. Maintain a daily teacher attendance log, and the concomitant records for substitute teachers.

23. Administer the early retirement program and retired employees insurance.

24. Is available to answer staff questions regarding Board Policy.

25. Is available to undertake any other assigned tasks from the Superintendent or Board of Education.

Terms of Employment:

Twelve-month contract. Salary and work year as per Board policy.

Evaluation:

Chapter
4

A More Detailed Look at the Typical Duties of the School Business Administrator

The school business administrator's duties and responsibilities are assigned by superintendent and/or school board. For example, whether construction management responsibilities are assigned to the school business administrator affects the number duties to be performed in the facilities management work/task area by this individual. On the other hand, school business administrators who are assigned responsibilities for transportation will have duties beyond those of some colleagues. In sum, duties derive from assigned responsibilities are dependent upon the district's size and organizational structure, as well as the management philosophy of the school board and superintendent.

How does the size of the school district, organizational structure, and management philosophy affect how school business administrators manage their programs? An obvious example relates to school district size. In large districts, school business administrators must divide their work and may delegate selected activities. Their duties may center on organizing, delegating, monitoring, and controlling those activities. In small school districts, the business administrator may be more directly involved with performing specific activities while delegating others. Said differently, in a large district the school business administrator may not have the time to directly manage every support service operation while in a small district staff limitations may dictate more direct involvement of the school business administrator.

The duties of the school business administrator also may vary with the type of school district organizational structure. In school districts with fewer students, the school business administrator often has responsibility for all of the district's business affairs. In others, school business affairs may be divided among several highly specialized professionals. For example, educational facilities planning, personnel management, data processing, grantsmanship, collective negotiations, and community relations are highly specialized areas that may be assigned to other professionals on the superintendent's leadership team. Thus, the school business administrator may either share or have little or no responsibility in these areas.

Similarly, individual school boards and the superintendent may have operating philosophies that affect the responsibilities of the school business official. If the superintendent especially enjoys school facilities planning, the school business administrator may not have direct responsibility for this function. If a school board is not sure that another member of the administrative staff can effectively manage a function like personnel services, the school business administrator may find him or herself in charge of this component of the district by default.

Clearly, the job definition of the school business administrator is complicated. Careful role delineation is essential since the potential of the school business program is extensive. Great care must be taken in deciding the responsibilities and duties assigned to the school business administrator in each and every school district. However, ultimately, while general duties will be similar, the role of each school business official is as unique and different as the district in which he or she works. The following provides a menu of duties that may be assigned to the school business administrator. Which ones the school business administrator actually assumes will vary as noted above. Note the "real world" differences in roles as depicted at the end of this chapter in the organizational charts of three school districts that vary greatly in size.

Typical Duties

While each school business official's job is unique, it is still important to have a broad overview of what the position can and does entail. To provide a broader understanding of the kinds of duties typically assigned to the school business administrator to other school officials and the public at large, a list of frequently performed functions is provided below. The list may be helpful to school board members, school administrators, and others concerned with establishing the position of school business administrator in a system that does not have one. It may also be useful in comparing existing responsibilities. Depending on district size, the following functions may be assumed by one person or assigned to several individuals.

I. **Financial Planning and Budgeting**
    A. Budget compilation, in coordination with educational planning
    B. Long-term fiscal planning/operating budget

C. Estimating

    1. Receipts

    2. Disbursements

D. Budget control

E. Fiscal relationships with other government units

F. Use of systems analysis and PPBES

G. Cash flow management

II. Accounting

A. General fund

B. Capital reserve funds, trust funds and special purpose grants

C. Construction funds

D. Internal accounts

E. Student activity funds

F. Voucher and payroll preparation

G. Inventory

H. Attendance, census, tax roll accounting

I. Government tax and pension accounting - categorical aids

J. Special trust funds

K. Cost accounting: cost analysis, unit and comparative costs, cost distribution

L. Student stores, bookstores

M. Source documentation

N. PPBES concepts and procedures

O. Employer benefits accounting: vacations, sick leave, seniority status

P. Petty cash funds

III. Debt Service and Capital Fund Management

A. Long-term and short-term financing

B. Maturities and debt payments

C. Long-range capital programs

D. Investments and cash flow

E. Reporting

F. Bond and note register

G. Debt service payment procedures

H. Short-term debt management

I. Revenue anticipation loans; emergency loans

J. Bond prospectus

K. Credit data, credit ratings

IV. Auditing

A. Pre-audit, or internal, procedures

B. Determination that prepared statements present the financial position fairly

C. Propriety, legality and accuracy of financial transactions

D. Proper recording of all financial transactions

E. Post-audit procedures

F. External audits

G. Reconciliation of internal and external audits

H. Legal advertising and reporting

V. Purchasing and Supply Management

A. Ethics in purchasing

B. Official purchasing agent designation

C. Legal aspects of purchasing and contracting

D. Purchase methods - seasonal and off-season buying

E. Stock requisition and buying cycles

F. Standards and specifications

G. Requisition and purchase orders

H. Purchase bids

I. Cooperative purchasing: state contracts, local contracts

J. Testing and value analysis

K. Purchases of supplies and equipment

L. Warehousing and distribution procedures

M. Storage, delivery, trucking services

N. Inventory controls

O. Management of supplies, furniture, equipment

P. Computerized purchasing and supply management

VI. School Plant Planning and Construction

A. Establishment of educational standards for sites, buildings and equipment

B. Plant utilization studies

C. Projections of facility needs

D. Design, construction and equipment of plant

E. Safety standards

F. Contracts management

G. Architect selection

VII. Operation of Plant: Custodial, Gardening, Engineering Services

A. Standards and frequency of work

B. Manpower allocations

C. Scheduling

D. Inspection and evaluation of services

E. Relationship with educational staff

F. Operation of related school-community facilities, such as recreation, park, museum, library programs, etc.

G. Community use of facilities

H. Protection of plant and property

I. Security and police forces

J. Salvage, surplus and waste disposal

K. Assessing privatization versus in-house delivery of services

VIII. Maintenance of Plant

A. Repair of buildings and equipment

B. Upkeep of grounds

C. Maintenance policies, standards and frequency of maintenance

D. Scheduling and allocation of funds and manpower

E. Modernization and rehabilitation versus replacement

F. Preventive Maintenance

IX. Real Estate Management

A. Site acquisition and sales

B. Rentals, leases

C. Rights-of-way and easements

D. Assessments and taxes

E. After school use of buildings

F. Dormitories, student unions, concessions

X. Personnel Management

A. Records

1. Probationary and tenure status of employees

2. Sick leave and leave of absence

3. Official notices of appointments and salaries

4. Retirement data and deductions

5. Salary schedules and payments

6. Individual earnings records

7. Withholding tax and group insurance or fringe benefits

8. Civil Service and Social Security

9. Substitute and part-time employees

10. Dues checkoffs

11. Benefits

B. Supervision of non-instructional staff

1. Recruitment

2. Selection

3. Placement

4. Training

5. Advancement

6. Working conditions

7. Evaluation

8. Compensation

9. Termination of services

C. Relationship to instructional staff

1. Good will and service concept

2. Cooperation in procurement

3. Cooperation in budget preparation

4. Information on pay and retirement

5. Personnel records and reports

XI. Permanent Property Records and Custody of Legal Papers

A. Security and preservation of records

B. Maintenance of storage files

C. Purging of records no longer legally required

XII. Transportation of Pupils

A. Policies, rules, regulations and procedures

B. Contract versus district-owned equipment

C. Routing and scheduling

D. Inspection and maintenance

E. Staff selection, supervision, and training

F. Assessment of utilization and evaluation of services

G. Establishing standards and specifications

XIII. Foodservice Operations

A. Policies, rules, regulations, and procedures

B. Staffing and supervision

C. Menus, prices and portion controls

D. Purchasing, storage and distribution

E. Accounting, reporting and cost analysis

F. In-service training

G. Coordination with educational program

H. Procurement and operation of contract services

I. Evaluation of privatization versus in-house services

XIV. Insurance

    A. Insurance policies

    B. Insurable values—buildings and contents

    C. Coverages to be provided

    D. Claims and reporting

    E. Insurance and procurement procedures

    F. Insurance and claims record

    G. Distribution of insurance to companies, agents and brokers

    H. Risk Management System

XV. Cost Analysis

    A. Unit costs

    B. Comparative costs

    C. Cost distribution studies

    D. Cost vs. benefit analysis of educational and operational options

XVI. Reporting

    A. Local financial and statistical reports

    B. State financial and statistical reports

    C. Federal financial and statistical reports

    D. Miscellaneous reports

    E. Required legal advertising

    F. Relationships with public information media

    G. Relations with other departments, the schools, and community

XVII. Collective Negotiations

    A. Service on management team when required

    B. Preparation of pertinent fiscal data for management team

    C. Development of techniques and strategies of collective negotiations

    D. Sharing of proper information with employee units

    E. Use of outside negotiations, agencies

    F. Mediation, arbitration, grievances

XVIII. Data Processing
    A. Selection of system
    B. Programming
    C. Utilization of systems analysis
    D. Forms preparation
    E. Broad use of equipment for all pertinent applications

XIX. School board policies and administrative procedures as related to fiscal and non-instructional matters

XX. Responsibilities for elections and bond referenda

XXI. Responsibilities for school assessment, levy\tax collection procedures as may be set by law

New Areas of Responsibility

Public Relations. Because of the complexity of our contemporary society, the school business administrator must view his or her role as greater than the functions, duties, and responsibilities actually assigned to the position. One new area involved in this expanded role is that of educational public relations. The school business administrator must communicate and interact with decision makers in the community because the school's business cannot be isolated from the community it serves. In recent years, taxpayers have become more knowledgeable about and concerned with the educational process and its financial operations. Therefore, it is becoming increasingly essential for the school business administrator to establish a direct line of communication between the school system and the public. These communications should be in conformity with guidelines established by the school board and the chief school officer.

The school business administrator must assume a prominent role in preparing and providing information to the public concerning school business operations. This type of community involvement can be of significant importance to the concept of school business administration and, when handled properly, can have a positive impact on community decisions on school operations.

In a community context, the school business administrator must recognize that the district and the schools are in fact part of the community. The educational system cannot be viewed as separate from the geographical, cultural, social, and economic context in which it operates. Therefore, the school business administrator must work to see that goals of the district are consistent with the larger goals of the total structure of the community. Sometimes this means that goals have to be change: sometimes it means that the school business administrator must help the community change.

Similarly, within a school system itself, sub-institutions can affect—and be affected by—the school business function. Therefore, the administrator must be aware that an interdependency also exists across the whole school system. Communication and positive relations with other segments of the school district are critical to the success of the business function and to the system as a whole.

Site-based Management & Privatization. School business officials today must also be prepared to deal with school-based management and privatization. In some school districts, the school business administrator has become both tutor and facilitator to principals as schools are assigned increasing direct responsibility—not only for curricular decisions—but also for how funds will be budgeted and expended. At the same time, many school districts are seriously considering or actively using contracted services as a means of delivering educational and support functions. More and more school business officials are finding themselves managers of contracts and liaisons between suppliers of services and the district itself. And in several states business administrators have been called upon to provide technical input on the efficacy of charter school applications.

Summary

In rapidly changing times most school districts are experiencing, educational institutions require a school business official who can do more than manage the traditional school business management components of budgeting and accounting. The standard business skills and abilities of the past are no longer sufficient. Today's school business administrator must learn new techniques and new approaches so that he or she can effectively and directly contribute to and strengthen the educational objectives of the community. This includes being effective in the are of human relations, public relations, technology, politics, strategic planning, and entrepreneurship. It also requires that a school business official be a lifelong learner.

Organizational Chart, Small District

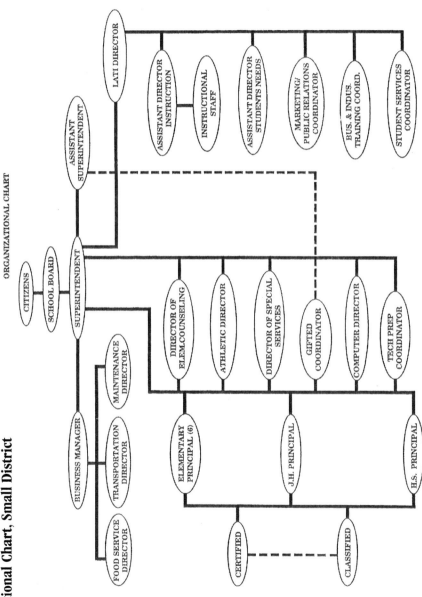

ORGANIZATIONAL CHART

Organizational Chart, Suburban District

ADMINISTRATIVE ORGANIZATIONAL CHART

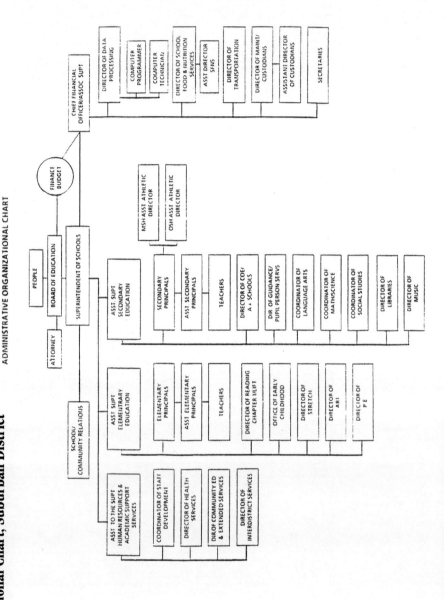

Organizational Chart, Large, Urban District

TABLE OF ORGANIZATION

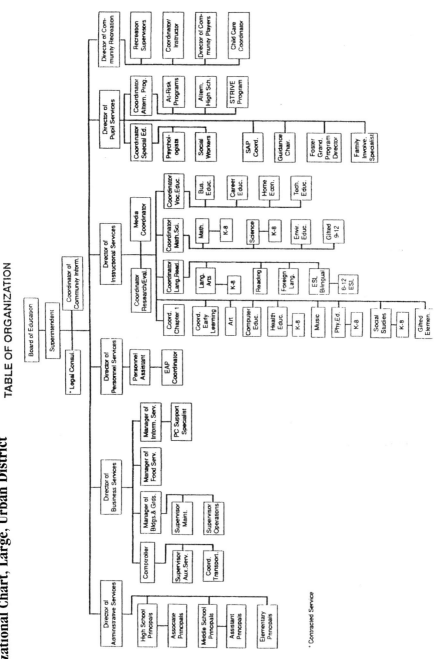

* Contracted Service

Chapter 5

What Should Be the Preparation and Experience of the School Business Administrator?

The school business administrator needs to be capable in business affairs, knowledgeable about educational problems, and competent in organizational effectiveness. His or her preparation and experience may be primarily in professional education with an understanding of good business practices or it may center in business with an understanding of the education field. The important consideration is the understanding that the job is that of business administrator *in* an educational enterprise.

To be truly effective, the school business administrator must possess high level skills in financial and general business management. At the same time, he or she must clearly perceive the probable effects of business decisions and procedures on the educational pursuits of the school organization. In essence, the truly competent school business administrator is highly skilled and knowledgeable in business functions but understands that support services exist primarily to ensure that students receive an effective education.

For several decades there has been controversy over whether the school business administrator should be a professional educator, or at least have had some experience as a classroom teacher, to have an understanding of the teacher's work. Similar controversies about executive background prerequisites exist in many fields. For example, should an automobile company president be a production man or a finance and management expert? Such controversies are not easily resolved.

In the past, some leading educators believed that some professional training and teaching experience were highly desirable. Even today some make it a requirement for appointment. Studies suggest that about three out of four school business administrators have had some educational experience. On the other hand, there are and have been many men and women who have achieved positions of responsibility and stature in the field of school business administration who have college training in such fields as business administration engineering, architecture, accounting, law, and other noneducational majors. Still others have achieved rank and responsibility primarily through long, successful, practical experience outside the education field and have then performed well in their education assignments. This is not dissimilar to successful school superintendents lacking specific education training.

The job is complex and requires both educational and business knowledge to be successful. The key to success is not so much how expertise is attained, but that the school business administrator has knowledge and understanding in both educational and business matters.

Initial Preparation

Because each school district and candidate is unique, no fixed set of qualifications or training will guarantee competency in a school business administrator. However, some type of formal professional program of preparation can provide knowledge and experience that will enhance the probability of success. The position of the school business administrator increasingly demands a high level of professionalism, including numerous and complex competencies and strong managerial skills. In contrast to the past, the majority of individuals who aspire to be school business officials today will find that school boards expect them to be college-trained and, in many cases, to have had previous professional experience, either in education or in business.

In certain collateral positions, such as those of school business officials having specialized responsibilities in plant operation, financial accounting, auditing, transportation, purchasing, data processing and energy management, college degrees may be outweighed by hands-on experience and training in the practical area involved. However, in most cases, preference usually is given to candidates having broad training as well as specialized competencies in a particular field.

In the past several years, many states and school districts have recognized the importance of preparing future and current school business administrators for today's rapidly changing and complex school district work environments. For instance, many communities and states have instituted vigorous programs of inservice education through conferences, workshops, and appropriate graduate study. In addition, ASBO has taken a leadership role in encouraging such increased specialization. The registration program outlined at the end of the first chapter is an example.

At a minimum, most school systems today require that an applicant for the position of school business administrator hold a bachelor's degree. School districts often expect that such degrees include study in at least some of the following areas: school business administration, general administration, school law, finance and accounting, school plant operation, planning and construction, school curriculum, management techniques, personnel work, and/or general education.

In many communities, no administrative posts will be assigned to candidates with less than a master's degree. Additional specialized preparation in certain areas may be expected as prerequisites for particular responsibilities. Preference often is given to those whose business training and experience are augmented by some aspect of education or teaching.

In this connection, it should also be noted that school boards, in selecting superintendents or chief school administrators, frequently recognize the special worth of those candidates who have knowledge of school business affairs. Many of today's outstanding school superintendents have had previous experience as school business administrators. Similarly, many school systems recognize the special worth of school business administrators who understand the importance of the educational program and its needs.

With respect to previous experience, studies indicate that very few school business administrators come to their position without prior work experience of some kind. Many have both education and business backgrounds. Generally, districts desire a minimum of at least three or four year's experience in business and/or education. In addition, most districts desire that a prospective school business administrator have at least some administrative or supervisory experience and responsibility. Preference is often given to those whose experiences have special value or application for the unique or particular responsibilities of a school system. For example, a person with an extensive capital construction background may be especially appealing to a school district about to enter into a long-term school building program.

Some states and districts require that the school business administrator be certified and/or registered. The intent is to assure districts that they are hiring candidates with at least the basic fundamental knowledge required to administer the business function of a school district. Two states' requirements are provide as examples at the end of this chapter.

Continuing Training as A School Business Official

Once in the job, the school business administrator often is assigned a wide range of responsibilities, making it difficult for any one person to keep informed of all the latest developments in various areas of responsibility of this position. The pace of change in educational procedures and management techniques is staggering. The introduction of highly sophisticated equipment, the electronic storage and retrieval of information and electronic formulation of knowledge, the transition from simple single-entry cash basis bookkeeping to complex electronic accrual accounting, zero-based budgeting, program level cost accounting, and many other changes, all have added new and complicated responsibilities to the office of the business administrator.

Continuing education programs are an important means for school business administrators to keep pace with rapid changes and developments. The type of program most beneficial depends on the incumbent's previous training and experience.

School systems need a coordinated and informed administrative team. Since the business administrator is a member of this team, keeping informed in all areas of school business management and finding ways for subordinates to keep informed in their specific field is a prerequisite for effective performance. Self-improvement should be considered more than just enhancing skills and knowledge in the business function. Keeping abreast of educational change also should be a focus of the school business administrator's professional development.

Continuing education for a school business manager may take many forms. Universities and college offer workshops, institutes, and short courses designed to cover specific areas relevant to effective school business management. Local, state, regional, and national associations and agencies offer a variety of staff development opportunities for the school business official. These opportunities are offered in a variety of formats including courses at higher education institutions, seminars at conference centers, and hands-on sessions at district offices by experts in particular fields. In many cases, professional development opportunities are made more convenient through technology, such as teleconferencing, the Internet, audiotapes, videotapes, and CD-ROMS.

State and provincial governments are yet another source of information and staff development for school business administrators. Most state and provincial governments provide seminars as well as printed materials regarding governmental procedures and regulations affecting school district operation. In addition, most agencies encourage individual school business officials to seek their help with specific questions or procedures.

A primary source of current information about leading-edge issues related to school business management are professional associations whose members are comprised of practitioners and other experts in the educational management field. The business administrator should be a member of such associations, should attend the meetings, should secure and read staff development materials of these organizations, such as monthly journals and other periodicals, and should take an active part in discussing with fellow members critical issues. One organization specifically developed to provide staff development for school business officials is the Association of School Business Officials International (ASBO). In addition, each state and province has its own local association of school business officials, which focuses on local or regional issues.

Summary

Changing times have brought increased complexities and a high degree of specialization in all areas of school business administration. Ever-increasing financial constraints and competition for the tax dollar call for ever-increasing effectiveness in the financial management and general business management of public school systems throughout the United Slates and Canada. It is imperative that school business administrators recognize the new dimensions of challenge and change that have increased their responsibilities and that they engage in the necessary pursuits of preparation and experience to meet the challenges and adapt to the changes.

New York State Registration Requirements

The University of the State of New York
THE STATE EDUCATION DEPARTMENT
Office of Teaching
Albany, New York 12230

AMENDMENTS TO THE REGULATIONS OF THE
COMMISSIONER OF EDUCATION

Pursuant to Section 207 of Education Law

80.4 Certificates valid for administrative and supervisory service (school district administrator, and school administrator and supervisor, and school business administrator).
A candidate may obtain a certificate for administrative and supervisory service upon evidence that the requirements of this section have been met.

(a) School district administrator (superintendent of schools, district superintendent, deputy superintendent, associate superintendent, assistant superintendent and any other person having responsibilities involving general district-wide administration excepting those responsibilities defined in subdivision (c) of this section, shall hold this certificate).

(1) Preparation.* The candidate shall hold a baccalaureate degree, based upon a four-year program of collegiate preparation, from a regionally accredited higher institution or from an institution approved or registered by the department and shall have completed in addition 60 semester hours of graduate study and an approved administrative/supervisory internship under the supervision of a practicing school administrator and of a representative of the sponsoring institution of higher education. Within the total program of preparation, the candidate shall have been awarded a master's degree. These 60 semester hours shall include 24 semester hours of graduate study in the field of school administration and supervision. An internship experience carrying graduate credit may be included within the 60-semester hour program. One year of satisfactory full-time experience in a school administrative or supervisory position may be substituted for the internship.

(2) Experience. Three years of teaching and/or administrative and/or

supervisory and/or pupil personnel service experience in the schools (N-12).

(3) Exception to stated preparation. The Commissioner of Education, at the request of a board of education or board of cooperative educational services, may provide for the issuance of a certificate as school district administrator (superintendent of schools) to exceptionally qualified persons who do not meet all of the graduate course or school teaching requirements in paragraph (1) and (2) of this subdivision, but whose exceptional training and experience are the substantial equivalent of such requirements and qualify such persons for the duties of a superintendent of schools. Prior to the appointment of any such individual the board must obtain the approval of the Commissioner. In its formal request to the Department the board must submit its resolution noting approval of the request, the job description, its rationale for requesting such certification of the individual, a statement identifying the exceptional qualifications of the candidate, the individual's completed application for certification, vita and official transcripts of collegiate study. The certificate, if issued, will be valid only for service in the district making the request. The Commissioner will refer the materials submitted by the board to a screening panel consisting of representatives of the Department and appropriate educational organizations for review and advice.

(b) School administrator and supervisor (principal, housemaster, supervisor, department chairman, assistant principal, coordinator, unit head and any other person serving more than 25 percent — 10 periods per week — of his assignment in any administrative and/or supervisory position excepting those defined in subdivision (a) of this section shall hold this certificate).

(1) Provisional certificate.* The candidate shall hold a baccalaureate degree, based upon a four-year program of collegiate preparation from a regionally accredited higher institution or from an institution approved or registered by the department, and shall have completed in addition 30 semester hours of graduate study and an approved administrative/supervisory internship under the supervision of a practicing school administrator and of a representative of the sponsoring institution of higher education. These 30 semester hours shall include 18 semester hours of graduate study in the field of school administration and supervision.

(i)   Substitution. One year of satisfactory full-time experience in a school (N-12) administrative or supervisory position may be substituted for the internship.

(II) Experience. Three years of approved teaching and/or administrative and/or supervisory and/or pupil personnel services within grades N-12.

(III) Time validity. The certificate will be valid for five years from date of issuance.

(2) Permanent certificate. The candidate shall have completed, in addition to the requirements for the provisional certificate, two years of school experience in an administrative/supervisory position. Within the total program of preparation, the candidate shall have been awarded a master's degree.

(c) School business administrator (deputy superintendent of schools for business, associate superintendent of schools for business, assistant superintendent of schools for business and any other person having professional responsibility for the business operation of the school district shall hold this certificate).

(1) Permanent certificate.* The candidate shall hold a baccalaureate degree, based upon a four year program of preparation, from a regionally accredited higher education institution or from an institution approved or registered by the department, and shall have completed 60 semester hours of graduate study and an approved administrative/supervisory internship under the supervision of a practicing school administrator and a representative of the sponsoring institution of higher education. Within the total program of preparation, the candidate shall have been awarded a master's degree. These 60 semester hours shall include 24 semester hours of graduate study in the field of school administration and supervision. An internship experience carrying graduate credit may be included within the 60-semester hour program. One year of satisfactory full-time experience as the chief business official of a school district may be substituted for the internship.

*   All persons shall have completed two clock hours of coursework or training regarding the identification and reporting of suspected child abuse or maltreatment. A listing of approved providers is available, upon request, from your local library.

Wisconsin Registration Requirements

CERTIFICATION REQUIREMENTS FOR
SCHOOL BUSINESS MANAGER

This classification shall apply to those who have been designated to have general responsibility for the administration of the business affairs of the district.

Certification of the School Business Manager shall be mandatory as of July 1, 1972, for the School Business Manager in any district having an average daily membership exceeding 1,500.

08   School Business Manager

For a regular license, the applicant must have completed and/or possess one of the following two minimum requirements:

1. A Wisconsin superintendent's license with three years of experience as a Chief School District Administrator in a district employing at least sixteen teachers, not including administrators.
                                or
2. a. A master's degree from an accredited college or University
    b. Nine graduate semester credits including such courses as:
        • school financial accounting
        • school business administration,
        • purchasing and supply management
        • school plant planning
        • personnel management
    c. Nine graduate or undergraduate credits in business administration including such courses as:
        • accounting
        • public finance
        • investments
        • insurance
        • public relations
        • data processing

      d.   Nine graduate or undergraduate semester credits in Educational Foundation area.

* Credit for equivalent courses may be approved by the State Superintendent.

Chapter
6

Procedures for Establishing or Restructuring a School Business Administrator's Position

Defining the Job

Once a school system has determined that the position of school business administrator is needed or should be restructured, the school board and the superintendent must determine the kinds of tasks and responsibilities that may best serve the school system. This must be done within the framework of local and statutory requirements and the nature and scope of the new or restructured position. Frequently, members of the school staff and lay citizens can assist the superintendent in identifying the specific areas important to the school system. Local business leaders are another good source of input on the roles and responsibilities of business managers in an organization. School business administrators in other communities may be able and willing to provide information concerning prevailing practices that may be helpful in establishing the most effective organization for this important position.

Before a school board establishes or modifies the position of school business administrator, it will want to verify the focus or purpose of the position. The board will want to know job expectations, the anticipated benefits, and the costs of adding or restructuring the position, as well as understanding its role in filling the position. Normally, the superintendent of schools is responsible for informing the school board, school staff, the public, and business community about the expected functions and responsibilities of a business administrator position. Then, the school board normally reviews and approves the position or changes to its existing responsibilities. With use of this open approach on the part of the superintendent, the school board will more readily be willing to employ or upgrade the responsibility of a capable school business administrator with little hesitation or restriction.

A fully qualified person in this position must be given latitude to administer the business affairs of the school entity within the policies, rules, and regulations established by the school board and within the accepted administrative practices of the district. The position must carry an amount of authority commensurate with the responsibilities. In essence, the school business administrator is a key professional in the total administration of the school system. Agreement between school board and superintendent about the authority and responsibility of the position is critical to the success of the school administrator.

Basic Steps for Establishing or Restructuring the Position of School Board Administrator

In general, the procedures for establishing or restructuring the position of school business administrator should include the following:

Define the tasks or the functions to be performed by the school business administrator. Preceding chapters of this monograph provide information in establishing general criteria on the scope of the work and functions to be performed by the school business administrator. Job descriptions from other school districts may also be helpful. Board, staff, and community discussions should then occur to determine the specific job tasks of the school business administrator based on specific local needs.

Establish (or affirm) the structural organization, lines of responsibility, and staffing of the school district. Provide in writing the rules and unequivocal delegations of responsibility, the school board and superintendent assign to the position of school business administrator. A component of this delineation is to define the organizational pattern necessary for the efficient and effective performance of administrative tasks. The board must conscientiously consider questions such as: "Who does what?" "For whom does the school business administrator do it?" "To whom does the school business administrator report?" "From whom does the school business administration take orders?" "Who helps with the task?"

Delegate authority commensurate with the responsibilities assigned. Few professionally trained people with a sense of integrity and pride in personal performance will wish to accept responsibilities for achieving goals unless they are also given commensurate authority to utilize the staff and other resources necessary to achieve those goals. Hence, the school board and/or the superintendent of schools should clearly define the extent of authority granted to the school business administrator for the achievement of assigned tasks. Friction, misunderstanding, and inefficient duplication of functions, not to mention wasted time, talent and energy, can be avoided when all concerned know the framework of responsibility and authority within which they work.

Provide for special assignments. Special conditions and situations may occasionally require that the school board or the superintendent of schools give the business administrator special assignments involving both instruction and business management. Provision must be made in the local rules, regulations, and job descriptions for establishing such assignments. And an understanding must be established as by whom and under what circumstances the job duties can or will be changed.

Specify qualifications of those holding position. Develop a list of required knowledge, skills, and experience. If the school business administrator is going to be heavily involved in the day-to-day operation and management of the financial aspects of the school district, the district will want to specify qualifications that are heavily business oriented. If, however, the position will primarily involve coordination, interaction, and communication, a candidate with a broad management background may best suit the district's needs. The key is to discuss and identify which characteristics are needed to fill the job before advertising it, otherwise, a district may end up with a great person who doesn't quite fit the job. In this case, everyone loses.

Defining selection process. Before the position is actually filled, all parties should have a very clear understanding of the selection process. The includes how the position will be advertised, who will be involved in the selection process, and how the final decision will be made.

Preparing a thorough job analysis, defining the job in writing, and specifying qualifications and experience to hold the position are critical to implementing or restructuring the position of school business administrator. Failure to determine expectations, how the position will operate within the system, and the necessary qualifications in advance will limit the school business administrator's effectiveness. Despite effort or expertise, individuals often fail in a position when the role of the position within the system was not well thought out. Careful pre-analysis is critical to successful implementation or reconfiguration of the position of school business administrator.

Obtaining an Effective Business Administrator

Once the school board and superintendent have assessed and structured the position, it's time to select a title and begin the search the right candidate. Although a vast number of titles are used throughout the United States and Canada, the most frequently used are School Business Manager, Assistant

Superintendent for Business Services, Assistant Superintendent for Finance, and Deputy or Associate Superintendent, and Assistant Superintendent for Administrative Services. Only after defining the job and giving it an appropriate title, should the district seek prospective candidates for the position. Once these are accomplished, the search begins.

Basic Steps in Selecting a New School Business Administrator

How does a school system go about the process of advertising for, recruiting, assessing, and selecting a school business administrator? There are several common steps any organization should take to select the best person for the job. These include:

Before advertising the job:

- Check board hiring policies.
- Confirm job description including qualification and salary range.
- Establish timetable for completing selection.
- Determine who will be involved in selection process.
- Verify steps required/desired to make selection. Determine if community input needed.
- Secure appropriate resources for the task including advertising and clerical assistance.

Recruiting:

- Commit all materials to writing including job description, selection steps, weighting of selection criteria, etc.
- Advertise — formally: newspapers, journals, etc.
- Advertise — other: universities, Internet, professional associations, school districts, etc.
- Advertise — individual: personally contact highly-regard school business administrators.

Selecting:

- Paper Screening - do applicants meet basic job requirements?
- References - are applicants recommended by those who should

know (verify by phone).

- Identify tentative pool for initial interview, contact to verify continued interest.

- Establish interviewing format, evaluation system (if not already in place).

- Confirm interview team or teams (such as district team, school-based team, community team, business leader team, or combination teams).

- Conduct the interviews under pre-established ground rules (time allotment, similar questions, etc.).

Narrowing Field of Candidates

- Use pre-established format for determining those candidates to be further considered (Weighting of input from various groups).
- Call additional references of potential finalists.
- Consider visiting the prospective candidate in his/her current work setting.
- Conduct second set of interviews as needed

Choosing

- Develop a summary of finalists listing strengths and weaknesses.
- Rank candidates for superintendent and school board.
- Indicate whether each applicant finalist, regardless of ranking, is a viable applicant.

Employing

- Secure school board approval of recommended candidate.
- Negotiate salary and conditions of employment with best candidate.
- Seek superintendent, then board endorsement or approval of condition of employment.
- Confirm board approval with candidate.
- Finalize the employment contract.

Other

- Announce the appointment (newspapers, in-house media, etc.).
- Formally introduce new employee to various constituent groups.
- Provide employee with orientation, induction, and general staff development.
- Notify all other candidates that position has been filled; thank them for applying.
- Evaluate your selection process for future reference.

Recruiting Tips

Obtaining the best candidate for the new position may require considerable time and effort. Several methods are available for filling new positions or finding replacements for existing positions, including recruitment from the field, training employees for promotion, and recruitment through universities and professional organizations. Each of these methods has its place in the selection and appointment of school business administrators. The following suggestions may help school boards and school administrators seeking to recruit a school business administrator.

Recruitment from within the field

The following techniques for recruiting within the field, derived from industrial recruitment procedures, can be used by school districts seeking executive talent:

- *Advertise the job in a variety of sources* including local newspapers, professional journal and publications, on-line employment job banks, conference job bulletin boards, etc.
- *Check with respected school business administrators in the field*. They often know of people in their own or other organizations ready to move up. Sometimes the administrator you call may be ready for a change or new challenge.
- *Check on employees currently in nonmanagement positions through personnel questionnaires, management evaluations, and personal interviews*. Potential executives may be discovered in entry-level jobs.
- *Check personnel files for applications and resumes submitted during the last year by persons seeking executive positions*. They undoubtedly are employed elsewhere now, but if they are qualified and still interested, they might be available.

- *Make the need known to other key school administrators.* Frequently another administrator will know of a qualified school business administrator seeking advancement to a more challenging position or an assistant in school business administration who is qualified for a position as a chief school business administrator.
- *Check with associates in county, regional, state, and national professional associations.* They may be aware of potential qualified candidates who may wish to apply for the position.
- *Check with business associates in the private sector for recommendations.* They may know of qualified individuals in industry whose management experience might make them excellent candidates. This must be done cautiously and at the risk of divulgence of confidential information.
- *Seek advice from other members of the administrative team.* They may know of qualified personnel interested in applying for the position.
- *Consider a Registered School Business Administrator or a Registered School Business Official.* Registration by the Association of School Business Officials International is excellent evidence of professional experience, satisfactory educational training, and ability. Contact ASBO for a list.

Promotion from Within

One of the chief sources of school business administrators will always be business officers and educators within the school system. Opportunities for promotion, upgrading responsibilities, greater opportunities for service, and increased earning potential will provide distinct attractions for eager employees. Any profession thrives when opportunities for growth and personal development stimulate movements within the field.

It is important, however, to have comparable standards for appointment for candidates from both within and outside the school system. Local availability, tenure, or political connections should not be accepted in lieu of competency or potential capabilities.

Many opportunities exist for a school district to fill a school business administrator position from its own management and supervisory personnel. Capable assistant superintendents in other areas, building principals, highly knowledgeable hourly employees, and supervisory personnel may possess the required attributes. Sometimes it may be easier to move a present employee vertically or horizontally within the school organization than to introduce a newcomer. However, should a district select a person from within the system, that person should be provided with all the necessary opportunities to succeed. This may include additional job training, formal course work, and/or mentoring relationship with someone highly knowledgeable in the field.

Recruiting is Everyone's Business

Finding and retaining an effective school business administrator is not an easy task. It is the responsibility of everyone associated with education to ensure that school districts have qualified people in the financial/support positions of the system. Without such people, school systems cannot operate effectively and efficiently. How can school systems and other related entities go about developing a corps of highly capable future school business administrators? Below are a few suggestions:

Prepare for orderly replacement of older personnel. Many school districts are aware of the approximate date of retirement of management personnel. Potential replacements can be trained as understudies to the experts now on the job. The trainee should be given opportunities to learn all aspects of the position and should be permitted to attend pertinent conferences and workshops. If the district anticipates hiring from outside, recruitment can and should be instituted before the job is vacant.

Introduce the educator to business administration and the business administrator to education. If a possible replacement or understudy for the position is an educator by training, the district should encourage the person to obtain additional preparation in business administration, accounting, and other aspects of management through university classes or self-instruction courses. If the potential replacement has come from industry, the district should urge him or her to take additional course work in such areas as the foundations of education, school administration, and school law. Professional and practical courses for school business officials are increasingly being offered by many institutions. Specialized workshops for school business managers and allied personnel are now available during the summer months. Thus, the dedicated school business officer who has been secured for a specialized field such as teaching or industry has many opportunities for further study and self-improvement.

Encourage participation in school business administration internships. Many school districts and universities cooperatively provide experience to graduate students as administrative interns in school business administration. Such an internship provides valuable experience and training to the intern. At the same time, it provides an opportunity for school districts and universities to evaluate the capabilities of the intern as a candidate for a position in school business administration. Districts should actively seek out participation in such internship programs. At the very least, the district receives additional assistance for little or no cost.

Recruitment through institutions of higher learning. Request folders of qualified candidates from universities that specialize in the preparation of school administrators for the position of school business administrator. Let them know the requirements of the position and the salary schedule so they can suggest desirable candidates.

Consult the local CPA (Certified Public Accountant) society. Frequently, the society will know of desirable candidates in other school districts or in industry who wish to make a change to advance themselves in management.

Check with local, regional, state/provincial, or national associations of school business officials. They may publish your position announcement in a monthly or bimonthly newsletter, and/ or may also have in their files the names of potential candidates.

Use ASBO International. Each month, *ASBO ACCENTS*, the Association's monthly news publication, lists vacant school business administration positions throughout the United States and Canada. This method has often been highly successful. It has not been successful when the position was clerical rather than administrative or when the salary range was low. However, for supervisory and administrative positions in the field of school business administration offering average or above average salaries, the response has been excellent and most responses have come from experienced persons in the field.

ASBO International Job Opportunities Booth. Since 1975, a job opportunities service has been operating at the Annual ASBO Conference in special sections of the exhibit area. Hundreds of available positions have been posted, covering such jobs as superintendents; deputy, associate or assistant superintendents; school business administrators; business managers; administrative assistants; and various business official posts in such areas as finance, facilities, personnel, foodservice, transportation, accounting, law, data processing and other specialized fields. Candidates seeking positions also may post their availability and job qualifications. Interested administrators and candidates frequently meet or arrange interviews during the conference period. The service is provided free of charge and is useful method of job recruitment.

Other Professional Association Job Bulletins. Such organizations as the American Association of School Administrators publish and distribute job announcements, listing many types of administrative positions. Some organizations also now have electronic job announcements provided on their World Wide Web pages.

Summary

School business managers have been recruited from the classrooms and offices of elementary and secondary schools, from universities and colleges, and from industry, commerce, business, and public administration. Previous work experiences often have included accounting, business administration, building contracting, insurance, purchasing, architecture, and school administration. Frequently the recruit has had work experiences in both school and nonschool situations. Business leaders, school superintendents, and school business officials emphasize that school business administrators should have knowledge of both the business and education function to be successful. Desirable experience, knowledge, and skills include finance and accounting, business and school administration, general management, education, human relations, politics and legislation, and communication. To recruit and retain a person with such diverse skills and knowledge takes planning and commitment.

Sample Job Announcement I

Assistant Superintendent, Business and Operations

The Position

ABC Unified School District is seeking an outstanding individual to assume the position of Assistant Superintendent, Business and Operations. The Assistant Superintendent, Business Operations reports directly to the Superintendent, is a member of his Cabinet and has responsibility for fiscal and planning services; information systems; nutrition services; purchasing and stores; maintenance, operations and transportation; risk management; internal audit; and, facilities.

About the District

Known throughout the State of California as a leader in educational planning innovation, the ABC Unified School District includes 19 elementary schools, five junior high schools and three comprehensive high schools. In addition, the district has a continuation high school, an adult school and a college prep 7-12 school. Supporting a diverse ethnic enrollment of 21,600, approximately eighty percent of the graduating students go on to higher education. The District has a $110 million operating budget and currently meets the State's minimum recommended reserve requirements. The district has passed a local bond and is implementing a $114 million facilities modernization program.

Duties and Responsibilities

The Assistant superintendent, Business and Operations provides district-wide leadership in the following areas:

- Assists the Superintendent in formulating district policies and/or administrating district programs.
- Proposes fiscal measures to maximize resources directed to the instructional goals of the District.
- Provides district-wide fiscal services, including assistance to other divisions in formulating their budgets, correlating all divisional budgets into a single district budget, disbursement of all funds and preparation of financial reports.
- Provides district-wide building construction services including the approval

and sale of bonds, site acquisitions, governmental approvals and construction of new facilities.

- Provides district-wide building/and grounds service, including the maintenance and repair of all buildings and maintenance of grounds.

- Provides district-wide food services; purchasing, warehousing and distribution of equipment and supplies; and, intra-office mail delivery.

- Supervises transportation services, including operation and maintenance of all school buses.

- Performs additional duties and responsibilities as delegated by the Superintendent of the Board.

Qualifications:

The successful candidate will have:

- Demonstrated administrative and supervisory abilities.

- Business Manager certification and/or minimum of three years experience in business and/or operations

- Consideration will be given to an administrative credential; a masters and/or a doctorate degree.

- Ability to analyze instructional program needs in light of fiscal constraints; prepare comprehensive reports, projections and display documents; prepare well defined recommendations or have the ability to define alternative courses of action for administrative decisions; supervise and motivate assigned personnel; interpret and comprehend school district laws and regulations; communicate effectively in oral and written form; and, maintain effective work relationships.

- Possess formal knowledge of business management practices, accounting and auditing practices and principles; data processing operations; methods of organization; financial control; and, governmental budgeting.

Salary:

The salary range is $94,000 plus $1,000 for doctorate or MBA plus a $3,500 district-paid tax sheltered annuity and a $250 monthly expense account. An attractive fringe benefits package is provided.

Application Procedure:

In order to open a file and be considered initially, the candidate must provide:

- A letter of application and resume
- A completed application form provided by the search advisors.

Following initial review, candidates may be asked for a copy of confidential placement papers and/or letters of recommendation as well as additional references.

All materials received will be treated confidentially.

The Tentative Selection Timeline

Submittal of Application   9/04/___
Completion of Paper Screening   9/09/___
Interview Candidates   9/16/___
Appointment by Board of Education   October 19___

Contact:

School Services of California (SSC) will conduct the search and recruit qualified candidates. Application materials must be received by SSC no later than September 4, 19___. Please forward application materials and requests for information to: .

Chapter 7

Compensating the School Business Administrator

The primary purpose of any good salary plan is to attract and retain the services of competent people. The applicant for a business administration position will, of course, evaluate a specific job opportunity in terms of additional factors such as administrative personalities and relationships, school-community attitudes, working climate, physical facilities, job status, community housing standards, cultural and recreational resources for family living, and potential opportunities for professional growth and promotion. Nevertheless, in our economically centered society, salary is of great importance.

The most recent studies of salary patterns for school business administrators indicate that the school business administrator is frequently the highest paid administrator after the superintendent of schools. Although not all school districts have established a salary schedule for business administrators, many districts provide salaries and raises according to patterns established for other school administrators. In some instances, the school board establishes the salary on an annual basis. In others, the school business administrator's salary may be based on an index relating to the teachers' salary schedule, taking into consideration months employed, years of experience, and education.

How are Salaries for School Business Administrators Determined?

The real answer is, "It depends." Some districts arbitrarily set the school business administrator's salary. This approach could result in excessive turnover, poor morale, and/or reduced job performance. Other districts institute salary compensation studies. In such studies the roles and responsibilities of the district's school business administrator are compared with those in other school systems. When like positions are found, the salaries are compared. The goal is to pay the district's school administrator a salary comparable to what he or she would earn someplace else.

Some districts hire outside professionals to conduct salary studies. Other school systems use employee teams to study salary structure and ranges. Sources of information for salary studies include salary information collected by state and provincial associations, state education department and state labor department salary data, and national data collected by such organizations as Educational Research Services (ERS). Professional Associations such as ASBO International, AASA, and NEA are also good sources of salary data.

While using national data can give an overall perspective on the monetary worth of the position of school business administrator, national studies may mask the wide differences that exist in different parts of the continent. Similarly, national data may not reflect the unique job requirements or availability of an employment pool unique to a specific state or region of a state. For that reason, most school systems find salary data from similar sized school districts in their region are more appropriate when deciding on pay ranges. However, caution should be exercised. If a district is the only urban one in the area, a fairer comparison may be to determine what other urban school districts in the region or state are paying. The key is to compare similar positions in similar economic settings.

Some Helpful Hints in Establishing Pay for School Business Administrators

While the issue of compensation can be an emotional one, and is usually specific to the economic and cultural conditions of an area, some guiding principles may help school districts develop fair compensation systems. Some general conclusions from past experience of school systems may be helpful to school boards and superintendents in determining salary schedules for positions of school business administration in their own districts:

Relationships to Teachers' Salaries. In some communities, the school business administrator's schedule has been expressed as a ratio to the teachers maximum salary. For example, a district may pay the school business official 1.95 times what he or she would make on the teacher salary schedule. The assumption is that the ratio represents how much more difficult the school business administrator's job is than that of teacher. The problem with this approach is that teacher salary schedules often revolve around levels of certification, education degrees, and experience in the classroom — factors often unrelated to qualifications of the school business administrator position. The use of the ratio or index plan for determination of administrators' salaries is declining. Many school boards feel that salaries of management personnel should not be based exclusively on the results of negotiated settlements with teacher associations or unions, particularly when administrators represent the board in negotiations.

Relationships to Superintendents' Salaries. In a few cases, the school business administrator has been paid the same salary as the superintendent. In most cases, his or her salary is determined in some ratio to that of the superintendent's. For example, an associate superintendent for finance position may be designated as worth 80 percent of what the superintendent makes. Again, this system appears to be in decline, the problem being how to determine and explain how the ratio is generated.

Relationships to Peers' Salaries. In more and more cases, the school business administrator's salary is determined based on comparison with professionals in similar jobs. This system seems to be more understandable and defensible to communities and school boards. With this system, the salary is described in terms of what other districts are paying to get the same job done. While such comparisons better reflect the reality of local and regional economic conditions, one concern is that in economically depressed areas, such an approach may preclude a district from recruiting an able person from a more economically vibrant region.

Salary Schedules. In many districts today, basic salary schedules provide step increases for experience and provide additional compensation for higher levels of educational training. Some salary schedules also provide incentives for outstanding performance. Some districts add them to the base salary, while others pay them as one-time bonuses. A growing phenomenon among school system policy makers is the desire to tie pay to performance. Some districts have done away with the traditional pay schedule. Instead, using the superintendent's assessment of performance, the school board provides individual raises to employees based on contributions to the school system in a given year. In these systems, the entry salary is often individually negotiated and any advancement is dependent not on a prescribed salary schedule, but with the superintendent's and school board's assessment and perception of individual job performance.

Compensation Other Than Salary

In a growing number of school systems, key employees such as the school business administrator receive additional perquisites beyond salary to compensate for the complexities of the job. These perks often include travel allowance or car, special vacation arrangements, tax sheltered annuities, added life insurance, more comprehensive health benefits, payment of professional organization membership fees, conference attendance allowance, and extended contracts—some with buyout features. These additional employment benefits often can make a job more attractive to a professional than the base salary. The differences in the extent to which perks are provided make it difficult to compare compensation across districts. While one school business administrator may make less in basic salary, he or she may in fact receive other benefits that make the job much more valuable than the salary schedule reflects. Any district beginning a study of compensation is advised to include a comprehensive assessment of benefits that include not only salary but also other perks, as described above.

Creating a *Fair* System of Compensation for School Business Administrators

Several years ago, the American Association of School Administrators and the National School Board Association identified seven characteristics of a healthy compensation structure that are still pertinent today. When looking at compensating employees, any school district would be wise to determine if the existing and/or proposed pay system accomplishes the following:

- Is it equitable—similar pay for similar job responsibilities?
- Is it rational—more pay for more responsibility, complexity?
- Is it competitive—ability to attract and retain competent employees.
- Does it retain—keeping turnover at a reasonable level?
- Does it recognize job performance—sensitivity to quality of work?
- Is it responsive—easy of adjustment for economic conditions?
- Does it provide career growth—development opportunities for employees within the system?

School Boards and school leaders are encouraged to include these attributes in the compensation plans of workers at all levels, and particularly at the administrative level where there are relatively few bargaining procedures available to top employees.

The Overall Salary Status of the School Business Administrator

Though the figures change from year to year and are often out of date by the time they are in print, several different national comparative studies made over several years show similar results. It appears that the school business administrator's salary is advancing comparably with the salaries of teachers and administrators, and in most communities that salary is usually among the three to five highest paid by the school system. Many districts feel that the school business administrator is the toughest position to fill and continue to reflect this in higher compensation levels for persons in that job.

Summary

Each community must determine its own salary ranges for school business administrators, guided by sound salary principles that promote good staff relationships, attract and retain competent persons, and promote increased efficiency and continuing educational benefits. These salaries should recognize the added complexity and responsibilities of tasks assigned to the administrator today.

There is a growing recognition that the position of school business administrator is one of the most valuable to the overall success of a school system. Pay levels today reflect this growing appreciation for the position. However, more and more school systems are demanding measurable outcomes for the pay an employee receives. While the average pay of school business administrators continues to rise, performance is a greater determinant than in the past.

Chapter 8

The Legal Implications in School Business Administration

Being well informed about the legal framework and limitations within which the school business administrator must function is critically important. Much of what is done in a school district is governed by law, legal precedent, and state and local policies and regulations. If the school business administrator is not fully prepared to operate within this context, he or she could very well be named in a lawsuit.

This chapter is not intended to be a mini-legal course, but rather an attempt to convince the practitioner, regardless of his or her experience, of the imperative need to be on sound legal ground in administering the duties of his or her office. Though not always crystal clear, the law must always prevail. The school system, as a public institution and agency, can afford nothing less than meeting the full requirements of the law—and these are under almost constant scrutiny and change.

The school business administrator must be fully knowledgeable about what the law is, stay constantly alert to changes in legal requirements involving his or her assignment, and be steadfastly committed to procedures that will withstand examination through litigation. Although there is a place for argument and interpretation, the school business administrator must not engage in speculation or gamble on his or her own ability to outmaneuver the law and the courts. To depend upon the plea of innocence because of ignorance of the law is not an acceptable excuse. The public will neither be sympathetic with such a defense nor be tolerant of such a level of incompetence.

Within the structure of administrators in a local school district, the business administrator, by virtue of his or her duties, is often in closest contact with laws and legal requirements pertaining to the operation of schools. Whether this condition comes about by specific assignment and job definition or by assumption in the normal course of events, it is a responsibility that cannot be avoided, let alone neglected. He or she must establish and maintain a communication system with all components of the district and with the community to let each know of the legal context of decisions and actions.

Today's demands on educational administration and operation leave little room to deny that in practice the school business administrator must serve as a quasi-legal representative. However, among the many skills of this professional, the school business administrator must know when to call for the services of a licensed attorney. There is no substitute for competent legal counsel, and school districts cannot afford to be without such services.

Legal Framework of School Business Management

The law can be described as a common reference point or framework within which school business affairs are to be conducted. Legislation from federal, state, and local government levels; judicial decisions from federal, state, and local courts; and policies and regulations from federal, state, and local school governing agencies provide both general and specific guidelines and procedures for many decisions and actions in school business matters. When the work/task areas associated with the responsibilities of the school business administrator are examined, it is readily apparent that the law undergirds most, if not all, of these operations and activities. For these reasons, it is of great importance to understand some of the legal issues and questions involved.

With litigation a common component of American life today, the demand on the school business administrator to know the law has thrust another major responsibility onto an already complex and demanding job. It is a fair generalization that, by comparison, the business affairs office of school districts often exceeds all other areas of the system in the extent to which laws, court rulings, and federal, state, and local regulations impact on decision-making and operating procedures. For a school business administrator to be effective requires not only an understanding of the legal context of school business management, but a continued monitoring of new legal precedents that impact on all school system functions.

Sources of Legal Impact

The sources of school law can be identified as (1) the constitution of a state or province; (2) statutes and enactments of the state or provincial legislature; (3) decisions of state or provincial courts (case law); and (4) codes and directives of authorities such as state or provincial school boards, as well as (5) federal statutes; laws; court rulings; and agency policy, rules, and regulations. Within this context, a local school district operates as an agency of a state or province and has only those powers expressly given to it. As such, the local school district is a quasi-corporation (involuntary). As a unit of government, the local school district is quite separate, in most instances, from the municipality or other political subdivisions of government in which it is located. In general, the local district is not subject to control or regulation by authorities of other units of government, unless such authority is specifically provided by statute. The school business administrator must always know what is permitted and required by statute.

It is obvious that what a school district does is directly affected by the broad dimensions of law. What is not always clear within this legal context, however, is the role of the school business administrator. The position has no inherent authority. School business administrators must work closely with their superintendent, school board, and school system attorney to define the legal parameters and extent of discretion the school business administrator is to operate within. Thus, an effective school business administrator is one who knows and understands how much legal authority and responsibility he or she is to assume directly—and in what cases authority and responsibility rest elsewhere.

Business-related Functions Impacted by Legal Considerations

The more common operations of the school business administrator that have strong legal implications and demand strict adherence to legal procedures and clear understanding of limitations and rights, are contracts, tax levies, debt limitation, allocation and management of school funds, the budget, elections, audit, property management, bidding, property use, transportation, a variety of state and federal reports and, fund borrowing. Other areas involving the school business administrator are bond programs, refinancing, tenure actions, liability litigation, condemnation, abandonment of property, right-of-way actions, zoning restrictions, inspections by municipal authorities and assessments. A growing area of importance related to legal requirements is personnel management, including such areas as hiring, dismissing, evaluating, the disabled, and workman's compensation claims.

The following delineates areas of responsibility for school business administrators as well as potential areas of litigation. The list illustrates the type and breadth of information the school business administrator must have to properly administer the responsibilities of his or her office. Above all, the list reinforces the idea that the school business administrator must be a scholar of statutory enactments of his or her state, as well as at the national level. He or she must recognize that the business of schools is a public trust governed by law, policy, and regulation.

School Board Meetings. The legal status of school board action has come into question a number of times. It is, therefore, important to understand the law as it applies in a particular state or province because of possible impact on school business matters. A school board can act only through the consensus of its members, for it is the school board and not the individual members that are given the power to act. Other litigation over board meeting issues has dealt with the legality of board meetings, written notice, the taking and counting of votes, quorum action, tie votes, a majority vote, finality of board action, closed meetings, and board minutes. These and other similar matters may affect both policy and actions related to the business affairs of a school district.

Elections. Local bond referenda and school millage elections are important to school business operations. The validity of elections is the subject of a great deal of litigation. Usually, however, the courts have been slow to set aside an election on the grounds that it was not valid. Court challenges have included the interpretation of statutes, election fraud, election petitions and notices, ballots and balloting, and majority votes.

Taxation. Most litigation in the area of taxation has been concerned with the levy, assessment, and collection of taxes. It is generally held that where a school board or other authority has tax levying authority, its actions are presumed to be legal, and anyone challenging its actions must bear the burden of proof. A school board, in assessing and levying taxes, is performing a quasi-judicial function. Board actions are upheld in the absence of proof of illegality, fraud, arbitrariness, or error. Other areas that have been subjected to litigation include the legality of taxes and disposition of tax proceeds and the assessment of property and collection of taxes. Clearly, this area is of considerable concern to the school business administrator.

School Organization. Most of the litigation in this area involves the interpretation of statutes, and there appears to be no general legal principles that have universal application. Therefore, it is clear that such legal problems or questions must be considered as a part of the law in a particular state or province. There appear to be two discrete areas of litigation: the consolidation of schools or attendance area reorganization and the merger of school districts.

Generally, the courts will not interfere with a school board's exercise of discretionary power to consolidate schools vested in it by the legislature or constitution except in cases of clear abuse of that power. Furthermore, unless evidence is presented that a school board has acted arbitrarily, capriciously, or illegally, its actions in reorganizing attendance area boundaries will not be interfered with by a court. However, it should be repeated that state/provincial and local statutes and state or provincial court decisions prevail in such matters.

Much litigation has been concerned with the reorganization of school districts. Courts generally agree that school district reorganization is a legislative function. School districts have no vested rights in their own existence and no property rights in the location of their boundaries. Other areas of litigation involve petitions for annexation; the creation of school districts; the constitutionality of reorganization legislation; the transfer of property; notices, orders and elections dealing with reorganization; competition for the same territory; and the legality of school districts.

A relatively new area receiving the attention of the courts and school and school district organization is use of alternative educational delivery systems. Home schooling, charter schools, and school choice using public funds are being addressed in various courts. What precedents, if any, will come from these cases is unknown. However, in an era of educational restructuring, the school business official is encouraged to monitor this emerging area of legal challenges and interpretations.

Budgets. School funds are state funds. The legislature may enact laws relating to school funds unless otherwise provided by the state constitution. The legislature also may enact laws that determine the method by which any school district may appropriate and account for expenditures. Control of budgetary practices is the domain of the legislature and the courts have protected that power.

Even though statutes may determine when and how budgets may be proposed, amended, publicized, presented to the public, advertised, and adopted, the courts have recognized the discretionary power of school boards to allocate funds to competing demands of the school program. The courts have dealt with other budget issues such as official appropriation, prior authorization, surplus funds, special funds, co-mingling of funds, student fees, emergencies, and transfer of funds.

School Debt. State legislatures impose limitations on school borrowing to whatever extent they deem prudent. It is clear that school districts have no implied power to raise funds either by short- or long-term borrowing.

Usually, the controls imposed on short-term borrowing are not as stringent as those affecting long-term indebtedness. Short-term borrowing is usually limited to anticipated revenues and is not subject to dollar limits of long-term debts since the annual budget and tax limits provide some protection. Long-term debts are used to finance school construction and other capital improvements. Dollar amounts and the procedures used to create the indebtedness are regulated by state/provincial constitutions and state/provincial statutes. The courts have dealt with such issues as validation of bonds, approval of bonds, creation of debt, legal defects, debt limits, and bond elections.

Contracts. Common law imposes a number of requirements on public contracts. These include legal capacity of parties, mutual assent, valid consideration, legal subject or content, and enforceable terms. The courts have dealt with such issues as pecuniary conflict, ultra vires contracts, contract awards, competitive bidding, bidder qualifications, withdrawal of bids, rejection of bids, bid alternates, and contract amendments.

Liability. A school district can act only through those persons whose conduct is imputable to it. Under the common law principle of "respondent superior," a master is responsible only for authorized acts of its agents; therefore, the conduct of an employee of the district could be imputed to the district if such conduct was within the scope of the employee's authority.

Issues that the courts have considered include negligence, nonfeasance, malfeasance, nuisances, governmental immunity, proprietary activity, discretionary acts, limits on recovery, procedural matters, and the liability of school officers. In recent years, cases involving civil rights, affirmative action, Title IX, violations of privacy, job discrimination, harassment, accessibility, and other areas of liability have markedly increased.

Insurance. State and provincial statutes will govern in establishing what shall be covered by insurance, the limits of insurance coverage, and the procedures for acquiring it. In the absence of statutory authority, the power to insure school property is implied from the general power that a school board possesses to manage school district property.

The courts have dealt with issues pertaining to school insurance such as group life insurance for teachers, construction insurance, workmen's compensation, liability insurance, and pupil transportation insurance.

The School Plant. School districts hold school property as trustees, not as owners. School property is subject to control by the legislature in that it may change the trustee at any time. The procedures by which school districts acquire, construct, operate, and manage school property are determined by state or provincial statutes. However, the courts have become involved with selected issues dealing with certain aspects of managing the school plant which include selection of school sites, the acquisition of property, eminent domain, school design, cost and financing of buildings, building code jurisdictions, reversion of title, contractor's bonds, special assessment for local improvements, defective performance of contractors, nonschool use of school properties and sale and lease of school property. Lawsuits involving the closing, proposed closing, conversion, or alternate use of school buildings are not uncommon.

   Transportation. In most states and provinces, statutes either authorize or require that school districts provide pupils transportation to public schools. The courts have dealt with these and other issues such as walking distance, bus routes, private contracts, district liability for pupil injury, bus driver negligence, and transportation insurance. In many areas, transportation to non-public schools has been authorized, mandated, and contested. Transportation of the disabled, as well as use of buses for senior citizen or adult activities, has also engendered much litigation.

   Personnel. The courts also have dealt with a number of pertinent issues involving non-certified employees. Some personnel issues in this area have included employee status, standards for employment, eligibility lists, dismissal procedures, oral contracts, tenure, retirement, and workmen's compensation.

   Purchasing and Procurement. State and provincial statutes provide litigation that seeks to prevent fraud, collusion, and favoritism and to enable public schools to receive the best in goods and services for the lowest available price. Litigation in the courts has dealt with such matters as the requirement for competitive bidding, contracts for goods and services, lowest responsible bidder, bidding practices, contract changes, bidder qualifications, withdrawal of bids, right to reject bids, and contract awards.

   Employee Negotiations. Litigation in the field of collective negotiations is still emerging and is on the increase. Many questions raised by statutes enacted by state or provincial legislatures regarding collective bargaining are yet unanswered. Annual revisions of public employee labor relations laws would indicate that there is not yet a set of common principles to guide collective negotiations. In many settings, the laws of each state and the court decisions pertaining to their interpretation must be examined in order to obtain an understanding of what the law is in each state. The courts have dealt with such issues as the legality and enforceability of collective agreements, the right to strike, the duty to negotiate, the rights to join associations, arbitration, unlawful work stoppage, injunctive relief, and union rights.

Gaining Knowledge of the Legal Context of the Job of School Business Administrator

One place to start is to become familiar with basic legal terms and principles. School law is both complex and broad, but not so complex that its basic principles cannot be understood. If a school business administrator has not already done so, he or she should take a course on School Law to provide a framework for understanding the legal context of education. In addition, the school business administrator should carefully review the laws, policies, procedures under which he or she is to operate. Further, the school business administrator should seek out input and assistance from state/provincial departments of education regarding required procedures. And the school business administrator should never hesitate to bring concerns or questions to the school system attorney.

Most of all, the school business official needs to have a clear understanding of the authority he or she is expected to exercise in the job. This requires substantial and regular communication with the superintendent and school board—and a clearly written and board approved specification of the school business administrator's authority, and its limitations. In any case, anyone who strives to be effective in guiding the business affairs of a public institution must have an underlying understanding of the legal implications of his or her duties. And, must work to establish an effective working relationship with the school system's legal counsel.

Summary

The position of the school business administrator is becoming increasingly diversified. More important than this diversification is the law that controls and governs our society and, in particular, those in positions of responsibility and public trust. Recognizing and respecting the legal implications surrounding school business administration is an imperative of school administration. Only those who recognize and function within the law can be totally competent and creditable in administering their duties.

Because the legal context of operating schools has become so complex today, however, a school business administrator must secure competent legal services for the school district. And the school business official must seek out legal perspectives on even the most apparently mundane of decisions. To do otherwise is to put the district and the administrator in jeopardy of enormous lawsuits, loss of reputation, and most likely lead to job loss.

Chapter 9

The Personal Characteristics of Effective School Business Administrators and a Code of Ethics

Because management involves getting things done through the efforts of others, the successful school business administrator is one whose personality, attitudes, and actions will reflect the dignity and worth of other individuals. Because such a professional respects his or her own integrity and competence, the administrator will reflect an attitude of confidence in the integrity and worth of others. The officer's personality traits will be similar to those of successful managers in other fields. Some of these noticeable traits are suggested below.

Basic Personal Management Characteristics

A successful school business administrator often is identified as one who has the following personal management skills and characteristics:

- *Has "directed" drive*. Exhibits high level of energy, staying power, and confidence. His or her drive is directed toward achieving the goals of the organization.

- *Likes people*. Exhibits a sincere appreciation for people as unique personalities. Truly believes that given an opportunity, individuals strive to do their best.

- *Gets along well with others*. Exhibits good communication skills, is willing to let others receive some of the credit, and considers himself or herself to be a member of a team.

- *Is a good listener*. Makes each person with whom he or she interacts feel important. As a good listener, he or she often restates or summarizes what has been communicated by another to be sure the message has been received correctly.

- *Is fair in dealings with others*. Exhibits an understanding of and commitment to the ideas of impartiality and equity. Works hard to be sure that decisions reflect what is ethically the best for all involved.
- *Establishes a good work climate*. Exhibits a strong desire to create a work environment with high morale and individual job satisfaction. Employees are viewed as co-workers or peers rather than as disinterested workers.
- *Is a self-starter*. Exhibits a penchant for being proactive, instead of reactive. Constantly seeks new and better ways to perform his or her job functions, without being directed to do so.
- *Possesses a high threshold of annoyance*. Exhibits an ability to stay focused on critical issues and outcomes when petty problems or minor distractions arise. Reminds him or herself and others what is important—and what is not.
- *Uses highly developed writing and verbal skills*. Exhibits a command of the language and its structure allowing the administrator to effectively communicate ideas and perspectives to a wide array of groups and individuals. Communicates simply, directly, and clearly whenever possible.
- *Is a problem-solver*. Identifies the important components of a problem, available alternatives, and the costs and benefits that may accrue from the alternatives.
- *Desires to improve*. Exhibits a drive to learn and know. Seeks out input and feedback regarding personal job performance, regularly engages in professional development, and regularly sets personal improvement goals.
- *Is a decision maker*. Exhibits a willingness to make the tough decisions. Though he or she seeks out advice and input from others, the successful school business administrator ultimately realizes that a decision must be made, and is willing to make it.

Basic Personal Characteristics

A good school business administrator must also possess appropriate personal attitudes and values. Since so much of what the school business administrator does relates to personal interactions, and because so much public trust is placed in the position, special attention must be given to personal qualifications. Two of the most important personal criteria for effective business administrators are:

- *Good character.* Strives foremost to do "the right thing"—as opposed to what is fashionable, politically correct, or most self-serving.
- *Integrity.* Exhibits honesty, sincerity, and truthfulness as the cornerstones

of his/her approach to dealing with others.
- **_Sense of Humor._** Strives to enjoy life in general, and has a sense of humor that helps others keep trials and tribulations in perspective.

The Essence of Personal Characters of a School Business Administrator

The school business administrator should be a part of a strong team rather than a strong person standing alone. The administrator must select able and creative coworkers, cooperate with them in a give and take relationship, and desire the efficiency and broad viewpoint that is possible when several first-rate minds are analyzing a situation.

The school business administrator shows respect in dealings with others. He or she respects others, first, because of a belief in the fundamental dignity and worth of every human being. Second, the school business administrator believes a person should be treated with consideration, not only for what the individual is, but also for what he or she might become.

School business administrators never forget that their power is delegated by others. This power can be exercised only so long as they use it in accordance with the spirit and purpose for which it was bestowed. Their authority is limited by their objectives and the interests and desires of those affected by their actions.

The business administrator must have an above average intellect. A school system can be no better than the level of thinking of its administrators. The school business administrator must have good common sense, the ability to teach and to talk convincingly and logically, the willingness to initiate action, the tact to use diplomacy, and must be approachable.

A successful school business administrator has a probing and questioning mind. The professional business administrator has the viewpoint of a scientist in running the administration, constantly appraising conditions.. He/she is not content with existing conditions, but seeks a better answer or a better way of doing things. School business administrators are those who are able to stand back, take a critical look at the organization and say, "This can be done in a better way," and then proactively work toward meaningful change.

A Code of Ethics for School Business Officials

Because school business administration is a profession, it must have a professional Code of Ethics. The status and importance of activities engaged in by school officers has caused the Association of School Business Officials

International to make a continuing study of the ethics of the profession and a commitment to the highest standards of conduct among school business administrators.

In that regard, every school business administrator should have a goal of exemplary and ethical behavior. Such behavior is essential to establish the professional status of the position of school business administrator. It is also essential for the school business administrator to provide leadership that can give ethical direction to an important program in the school district. Thus, the school business administrator is a role model for the district and the community, setting the tone for what is and is not acceptable professional and personal behavior.

ASBO has recognized the importance of professional ethics. A code of ethics for school business administrators was listed in Bulletin 21, in 1960. The Code has periodically been reviewed and revised. Many state and provincial associations have adopted similar codes as guiding principles. Current and future school business administrators are encouraged to acquire and review these Codes.

The Association of School Business Officials International Code of Ethics believes in and supports the following:

A Commitment to Seven Standards

ASBO International firmly believes that school business administrators must strive at all times to embrace and operate within seven basic ethical standards. In performing their duties the school business administrators must do so in a manner that is:

I.   *Best for the Student*

The ultimate objective of all actions and decisions must be to give the pupil the opportunity to develop mentally, physically, socially, and morally to the fullest extent of his or her capabilities.

II.   *Fair to All Concerned*

The acceptance of personal responsibility and respect for the rights of others must be a basic philosophy in all actions. All facets of responsibility shall be administered in a manner to provide justice at all times with a realization that satisfaction for all is not always possible, to act with objectivity and impartiality, and to do everything to advance this standard.

III. ***Designed to Build Goodwill and Better Understandings***

The development of appropriate well-defined policies concerning communications, public and interdepartmental relationships, employee conduct, discipline, and welfare, along with the constructive implementation of these policies, is the basis of a sound public, student, and employee relationships. The result should provide the broadest opportunity for the development of goodwill and better understanding.

Mutual and honest information exchange between the individuals concerned, wherein confidential information is guarded and public information is not concealed, is the basis of confidence in operation.

IV. ***Based upon Respect for the Past, Knowledge of the Present, and Concern for the Future***

The realization of the richness in legacies left by predecessors and use of efficient methods based upon both these experiences and present ideas, leads to strengthening education in the present and in the future. Valid research methods are sound bases in building for the future.

V. ***Legally and Morally Right***

The conformance to all laws is the foundation of integrity of operation. Procedures must support only that which is legitimate under the spirit and letter of existent pertinent law.

Stewardship of the school business official is one of public trust, and duties must always be performed in accordance with the highest moral and ethical standards that will bring honor and credit to the school district.

VI. ***True to One's Conscience and Recognizes the Importance of Loyalty to Associates, to School District, to State, or Province and Country.***

The administrative staff of a school district is a team with a common goal always directed toward better education of youth. Cooperation with and loyalty to the team is essential for the achievement of this goal.

Loyalty to democratic ideals directed towards the goal of better education for youth must also include loyalty to the community, state, province, and nation.

The responsibility of stewardship and careful handling of public funds may be accomplished only by the conscious application of our highest abilities.

VII.   Supportive of the Concept of Performing at One's Best

A basic philosophy of service must be that the schools will be served by the best— in skills, in competence, in attitude, in personal qualifications, and in loyalty.

There must be recognition of a constant obligation to perfect knowledge of the disciplines of public school administration and skill in their application. The highest professional ideals in performance shall always be the challenge—to be met boldly through the implementation of new techniques, based upon proven research, that will provide the best ultimate tools for education.

As part of this commitment to quality, the school business administrator will:

- Reward merit on the part of subordinates and to reject all other approaches to advancement.
- Be unequivocal in safeguarding confidential information and not to profit unfairly therefrom.
- Applaud the accomplishment of peers and co-workers.
- Act firmly, fairly and quickly on the basis of fact, in cases of misconduct or neglect and to defend as firmly, fairly and quickly, those unjustly accused.

Ethical Commitment

In addition to embracing the seven basic ethical standards noted above, the school business administrator is expected to:

- Uphold the integrity and honor of the profession and to so conduct him or herself as to reflect credit upon the profession and inspire the confidence, respect, and trust of his employer, his colleagues, and the public.
- Accept the responsibility of his or her professional status.

- Support organized professional activities by devoting time and effort as his or her position and his ability reasonably permit.
- Participate in educational research and publish the results of such research.
- Support the premise of truth and justice that requires a code for ethical conduct.
- Unhesitatingly require the removal and/or disbarment of any colleague whose conduct is a reproach to the profession.
- Periodically review the ethical requirements of the profession and upgrade them as necessary.
- Foster mutual respect and understanding between public education and other segments of society.
- Maintain loyalties on the following priority scale: to the people first, and then to the organization, its members, and self.
- Procure employment on the basis of qualification and honest credentials; to apply for open positions only; to compete fairly with other candidates for those positions; and to reject the premise that to apply for another position as a means to advance one's present position, either in salary or status, is an acceptable tactic.
- Perform to the best of one's ability for the duration of a contract or agreement or until one has been released from such obligation.
- Keep abreast of developments in appropriate areas of education, but especially in those affecting school business administration.
- Promote professional growth of colleagues and self through affiliation with international, national, state, and local professional organizations.

Further, within the business community, the ethical administrator seeks to:
- Promote his or her reputation for honesty and integrity by accepting no gratuities, favors, or gifts that might impair or appear to impair his professional judgment.
- Exhibit loyalty to the community and the school district.
- Exhibit faith in the profession.
- Deal justly and honorably with all on legitimate enterprise.
- Consider first the interests of the Board of Education and to believe in and carry out its policies.
- Encourage the exchange of collegial counsel and to be guided by such counsel without impairing the dignity and responsibility of the office.

- Transact all business without favor or prejudice.
- Strive consistently for better knowledge and information on which to base decisions.
- Establish acceptable practical methods for the conduct of business.
- Denounce all forms and manifestations of bribery.
- Accord a prompt and courteous reception, insofar as it is possible, to all those who call on a legitimate business mission.
- Respect obligations and to require such respect consistent with good business practice.
- Avoid sharp practice.
- Enhance the quality and standards of the office in respect to specifications and the adherence thereto by all seeking to do business with the school district.

Summary

Unfortunately, in every field, there are those who will disregard ethical behavior because of either ignorance or personal gain. School business administrators should encourage state associations and local groups to be concerned with the implementation of exemplary practices. The school business administrator should provide leadership to encourage staff members to practice exemplary behavior every working day. The opportunity to serve as school business administrator should be used to build a reputation of exemplary conduct that will far outlast the tenure of the office. It is the opportunity to leave a legacy beyond the clarity of financial statements, the credibility of fund balances, or the toughness of fiscal decisions; it is to leave a legacy of exemplary behavior and unquestioned ethical conduct. The school business administrator truly is one of the key role models for everyone associated with a school district.

Chapter 10

Evaluating the School Business Management Function

The need for effective evaluation of the performance of the school business administrator becomes increasingly important as the pressures of the economy, fluctuating enrollments, reduced trust in public officials, and concern as to effectiveness of the public schools bring educational accountability to the forefront of public thought and discussion. Possibly more than any other time in history, legislatures, businesses, and communities are asking, "Are our schools effective? Are we getting the educational productivity commensurate with the resources we are putting in? Do we have the right people running our schools?"

School business administrators are the focal point of these questions for two reasons. First, school business administrators often have the information and data to answer the questions. Second, school business administrators traditionally have been viewed by the nonschool community as objective and trustworthy. A critical question for school boards becomes, "How do we assure ourselves and others that we in fact have a school business administrator who is professionally knowledgeable and also able to build and retain trust not only with the school board but the community at large?" One answer is to hire the best person a district can find. Ways to do this were discussed earlier in this monograph. Another answer is to specify job expectations for the school business administrator and then evaluate the performance against these pre-established standards or benchmarks.

How does a school district do this effectively? By specifying in writing what the school district expects from the school business administrator, how performance against expectations will be measured, and when, where, and how evaluation will occur.

Delineating Job Responsibilities

A basic ingredient of a successful evaluation process is careful delineation of the areas for which the school business administrator will be held accountable. It is fundamentally unfair to criticize a school business administrator for poor performance in an area for which the administrator was not directly informed he or she would be held accountable. The broad job tasks outlined earlier in this monograph may serve as a starting point to develop a listing of job assignments to which the school business administrator will be held accountable.

Establishing Authority to Perform Job Assignments

As important as designating areas of responsibility and accountability is providing the individual with the power and authority to get the job done. For example, if the school business administrator is held accountable for upgrading technology in schools, but individual schools maintain control of what they buy, the school business administrator may be criticized unjustly. Similarly, if the school board holds the school business administrator responsible for improving the physical condition of schools but sets aside no funding for capital projects, an unfair set of expectations has been placed on the him or her.

Establishing Indicators of Performance

It is one thing to say that the school business administrator is going to be held accountable for various operations of the school system. It is quite another thing to specify the indicators for success. It is critical that the school board and the school business administrator mutually agree on what constitutes adequate job performance. Without this prior agreement, even the best of intentioned school boards and school business administrators may end up in conflict. For example, if the school board merely states that the school business administrator is responsible for operating an effective school foodservice program, does that mean that the program should make a profit, or does it mean that student participation will increase, or that employee turnover is reduced? It is very possible that a school business administrator could be pleased with his or her performance while the school board is not for no other reason than misunderstanding of expectation.

Goal setting between the school business administrator and the school board (via the superintendent if that is the normal procedure) before a new fiscal year begins is one the most important steps in successful evaluation.

Confirming Evaluation Procedures

Once tasks and indicators of performance are clearly established, the next step in successful evaluation is to define how the evaluation process will actually occur will be needed to complete the evaluation. While this will vary widely by district, basic steps often included in an evaluation cycle are pre-conference (goal setting), formative evaluations (status reports of progress), and summative evaluation (formal determination of year's performance). The formative evaluations are particularly important to a good evaluation system. They permit the employee (in this case the school business administrator) an opportunity to hear whether he or she is making satisfactory progress toward agreed upon goals. If not, the school business administrator can adjust his or her performance. In any case, the administrator will not be surprised at the end evaluation if several formative evaluations have already indicated areas of weakness.

Evaluation Forms, etc.

How does a school district record the process and product of evaluation? There probably are about as many evaluation forms as there are school districts. The key is to have a form that delineates the tasks on which the school business administrator will be evaluated, the agreed upon indicators of success, and specification of any documentation required to substantiate that the indicators successfully addressed. Some districts use a checklist approach while others use a more qualitative system where goals, etc. are specifically developed and recorded for each administrative employee. There is not an absolutely best or fool-proof system. A district should choose one that it feels provides sufficient information to assess employee performance, is understandable to employees, and is as simple as possible to administer.

Purpose of Evaluation

An evaluation is not an end unto itself. It can and does serve several purposes. A key to successful evaluation is knowing what the evaluation will be used for. In some districts, unfortunately, it is used for little more than adding paper to personnel files. In other districts it has been used inappropriately to get rid of an employee who performed his or her job well but had ended up on in the political doghouse of the school system. A school board should formally establish the purpose of employee evaluations. Are they to be used to make reappointment decisions, to determine promotions, to determine base pay increments, to identify outstanding employees for incentives, to encourage professional growth in skills and knowledge, or a combination of these and others? Unless a district knows beforehand what it wishes to accomplish with an evaluation process, the most carefully design evaluation forms and procedures will be of little value or assistance.

Summary

Evaluating the school business administrator is one of the most important personnel functions a school board and superintendent perform. Therefore, it is imperative that such evaluations be fair both to the system and the school business administrator. It is the responsibility of the school board and superintendent to have the best possible individuals in critical positions such as school business administrator. A good evaluation system can help accomplish this. By the same token, it is the responsibility to treat the school business official fairly in the process. This means that a good evaluation system includes a clear understanding among all involved of what the job tasks are, what measures will be used to judge success, and the consequences of various levels job performance.

Finally, it is just as important for the school business administrator to implement a similar system of evaluation for his or her own employees. Just as school business administrators should expect to be treated fairly and professionally, all employees deserve the same consideration.

HARRISON SCHOOL DISTRICT NO. 2

Performance Objective

Employee:_____   Evaluator:_____

Assignment:_____   School Year:_____

Instructional Conference Date:_____

Performance Objective Type:
   (Check One)   ☐ Improvement   ☐ Remediation

Performance Objective:

Plan of Action:

Specific Assessment Criteria and Timeline:

Distribution: White - Evaluator   Employee:_____   Date:_____
            Yellow - Employee   Evaluator:_____   Date:_____

Form 01-9863   Rev: 7-93

Performance Objective
Summative Year-End Conference

Employee:_____   Evaluator:_____

Assignment:_____   Site:_____

School Year:_____   Date:_____

_____
EXTENT TO WHICH OBJECTIVES WERE ACCOMPLISHED
_____

Observation/Conference Dates: _____/_____/_____/_____

Performance: [ ] Meets District Standards   [ ] Does Not Meet District Standards
(Check One)

Performance Comments: Identify specific Strengths or Weaknesses

SAMPLE

_____
Future Action: [ ] Improvement Plan   [ ] Remediation Plan
_____

Employee:_____   Date:_____
    Signature does not necessarily mean
    agreement with this report

Evaluator:_____   Date:_____

Evaluator's
Supervisor:_____   Date:_____
    The Supervisor's signature on this
    form verifies that the report has
    been reviewed and that the proper
    procedure appears to have been followed

Distribution: White (Evaluator)
                 Yellow (Employee)
                 Pink (Evaluator's Supervisor)

Form 01-9865

I.   PLANNING/ORGANIZATION

   A.   Assists staff in establishing meaningful
         goals, objectives and concepts.
   B.   Takes initiative to develop and implement
         long and short range plans that will
         achieve district and departmental goals.
   C.   Is resourceful and creative in achievement
         of district and departmental goals.
   D.   Demonstrates organizational skills.

II   DECISION MAKING; TASK COMPLETION
      AND FOLLOW THROUGH

   A.   Utilizes problem solving skills
         successfully.
   B.   Accepts responsibility for own and
         subordinates' actions.
   C.   Decisions consistently reflect a knowledge
         of and support for Board Policy,
         Administrative Procedures and Operational
         Directives.
   D.   Decisions reflect consideration of available
         data and the ramifications of the chosen and
         alternate courses.
   E.   Provisions are made for appropriate staff
         involvement in the decision making process.
   F.   Monitors responsibilities delegated to
         subordinates to assure successful completion.
   G.   Follows established channels to achieve
         objectives.
   H.   Is industrious and diligent in task
         completion.

III. RELATIONSHIPS

   A.   Is available to staff for consultation.
   B.   Communicates effectively with staff and
         supervisors.
   C.   Is respected by supervisees and supervisor.
   D.   Interpersonal conflict is minimal and directed
         to issues rather than personalities.
   E.   Recognizes and reinforces departments and
         staff members when performance has been
         outstanding.

IV.   EVALUATION/ASSESSMENT/IMPROVEMENT

   A.   Seeks to assess and evaluate each program,
         task or process in his/her area of
         responsibility and to make necessary changes
         and improvements.
   B.   Actively participates in improvement of
         district and area of responsibility.

V.   PROFESSIONAL CONDUCT

   A.   Supports and utilizes district adopted
         curricular/subject matter materials or
         professional materials for which he/she has
         responsibility.
   B.   The administrator's relationships with
         appropriate district staff, appropriate
         building staff, students, and patrons shall
         be a positive one, characterized by honesty
         and integrity.
   C.   Is familiar with current educational
         research/thinking in his/her area.
   D.   Interprets the district program and policies
         to the community.
   E.   Promotes a positive image for Harrison
         School District.

HARRISON SCHOOL DISTRICT NO. 2

Instructional Conference
Central Office Administrative Staff

The following items are to be specifically included in the planned program of improvement for all certificated employees.

1. Evaluative criteria: (as listed on the back of this form)

2. Additional evaluative criteria as specified below:

    a) _____

    b) _____

    c) _____

3. Performance objectives as established between the employee and evaluator.

4. A review of the appropriate job description.

5. The procedures for conducting subsequent year-end conference report have been explained to the employee.

_____   _____
Employee   Evaluator

_____   _____
Date   Date

Distribution: White - Evaluator
                   Yellow - Employee

Form 01-9861

HARRISON SCHOOL DISTRICT NO. 2

Summative Year-End Conference Report

Employee:_____   Evaluator:_____

Assignment:_____   Site:_____

School Year:_____   Date:_____

This form will be completed by the assigned Evaluator for the summative year-end evaluation conference. All items must be completed and distributed as indicated below.

1.   The overall performance of this employee is:

      [   ] Satisfactory   [   ] Unsatisfactory

      Any employee rated as unsatisfactory must complete the attached remediation plan as outlined on a performance objective form.

2.   Specific evaluative criteria have been identified as "does not meet District standards":

      [   ] Yes   [   ] No

      If the answer to the above is yes, the evaluator must identify the specific evaluative criteria and complete a(n) improvement/remediation plan on the statement of performance objective form.

3.   One or more performance objectives have been identified as "does not meet District standards":

      [   ] Yes   [   ] No

      If the answer to the above is yes, a specific performance objective for improvement/remediation must be attached on the statement of performance objective form.

     Employee:_____   Date:_____
                  Signature does not necessarily mean
                  agreement with this report

     Evaluator:_____   Date:_____

Evaluator's Supervisor:_____   Date:_____
                  The Supervisor's signature on this
                  form verifies that the report has
                  been reviewed and that the proper
                  procedure appears to have been followed

Distribution: White   - Evaluator
              Yellow   - Employee
              Pink   - Evaluator's Supervisor
              Goldenrod - Director of Human Resources

Form 01-9864

Lower Camden County Regional High School District #1

Administrative Job Targets
School Year 19____

Category: *MANAGEMENT*

A.   Statement of Goal/Objective:

Continue the development of a Procedures Manual which clearly and concisely outlines procedures an employee should follow when conducting daily tasks required by their work.

B.   Plan:

As the procedures are written, have them reviewed by an appropriate administrator, assistant or secretary for corrections, deletions or additions. Have the proposed manual reviewed by the Superintendent for comments, corrections, deletions, additions. Have manual adopted by the Board of Education.

C.   Timelines

The formation and writing of the procedures manual will be completed by April,
The procedures manual committee met in July to discuss the format of the revised manual. The manual will be updated to include procedures for the business management of Lower Camden County Regional District #1.

Sections of the manual have been distributed to those individuals who are responsible for a designated activity. Approximately half of the manual has been reviewed and retyped as of this date.

D.   Progress Report - November, '

A meeting of the procedures committee was held on September 15, 19__. Participants are reviewing sections of the proposed manual. Progress is slow, but moving in the right direction. The first sections of the manual are being typed as of this date.

Progress Report - February, '

The development of the procedures manual is moving in the right direction. I am halfway through writing the procedures and intend to have it nearly complete by the end of April. I am receiving a great deal of help from the school secretaries. They have provided updated and revised procedures they are using at the schools. When all of their computers in their offices have been upgraded they will be able to have forms that are the same for each procedure followed at the school level. The procedures at district level are being reviewed by each individual who handles a particular task; such as payroll, purchasing, receiving, petty cash, student activity, mileage, etc.

Progress Report - May, 19__

The procedures manual is completely retyped. The next step in the process will be to have it reviewed by key individuals who will critique the document. Their suggestions for additions, deletions and/or changes will be made prior to presentation to
will have the opportunity to review and make suggestions for changes, additions, or deletions. Following the review and appropriate changes made to the manual it will be presented to the Board of Education for approval. The target date for Board approval is December, 19__.

The development of the procedures manual was _____ ve i _. It has taken the better part of two years to complete. I feel confident th __ __ __ __ will __ a worthwhile tool for administrators and their staff when han __ __ __ v __ __ __e __ an __ __ unctions required by State Law/Guidelines.

_____X_____Goal/Objective Met

_____Improvement Needed (PIP)

_____   _____

Administrator   Supervisor

_____

Date

Administrative Job Targets
School Year 19____

Category: *MANAGEMENT*

A.   **Statement of Goal/Objective:**

Budget Development Procedures and Progress

B.   **Plan:**

To continue to improve the format of the district budget/spending plan which permits budget planners to prepare a clear, concise, flexible spending plan for the district.
Encourage the Board of Education to change the format of budget reporting and improve the presentation of budge transfers.

C.   **Timelines**

Prepare documentation for the year and begin demonstrating a different format for budget and financial reporting November 1 __

The completion of this object e April, 19__ .

D.   **Progress Report - November, 19 __**

The budget preparation documents were submitted to the principals and administrative staff in September, 1997.

The CSI computer program provided the budget managers with a list of expenditures through June, 1997 and year to date through September, 19__.

The accounting department was also able to provide budget forms which will make the input of budget information much easier for the budget managers.

Progress Report - February, 19__

This objective is complete. The budget process proceding in very smoothly this year. There was very little confusion on the part of the budget managers (principals). They were received in a timely fashion and only two meeting were needed to check equity between schools and finalization. The Board adopted the budget as proposed in March. Next year I intend to have the process be more effective and to provide very little discomfort and uneasiness for those who are required to provide the district office with their spending plans.

Progress Report - May, 19__

The annual school budget did not receive approval by the electorate. A committee consisting of two Board Members, the Superintendent, and Business Administrator met with the mayors from six of the seven municipalities. After a short meeting an agreement was reached to cut the regional budget by $150,000. The Board of Education adopted the revised budget on May 18th, 19__. As of this date the spending plan for 19__ has been entered into the computer system and is ready for operation July 1, 19__. There should be no impact to educational programs resulting from the cut made by the municipalities.

_____X_____ Goal/Objective Met

_____ Improvement Needed (PIP)

_____
Administrator

Su_____c

_____
Date

Lower Camden County Regional High School District #1

Administrative Job Targets

School Year 19____

Category: *MANAGEMENT*

A.   **Statement of Goal/Objective:**

To establish a Hiring Procedures and Practices Policy

B.   **Plan:**

To have a Hiring Procedures and Practices Policy approved by the Board of Education which meets all the laws and regulations related to Hiring personnel

C.   **Timelines**

Seek approval of the Policy from the ~~the~~ by ~~November~~, 19___
Seek Board of Education approval in ~~~~
Implement the policy in January

D.   **Progress Report - November 1__**

The proposed Hiring Procedures and Practices Policy was reviewed with
in September. A sub-committee of the original committee met in September and reviewed the suggested changes made by   . The committee reviewed and approved the changes on October 14, 19___. The proposed policy and procedures, with all of the changes made, is being typed and formatted by   . The final document will be presented to
in November, 19___.

Progress Report - February, 19__

This objective is complete. The Board of Education adopted the Hiring/Procedures Manual on February 23, 19___. The payroll department and risk management departments will be restructured as of July 1, 19___ and we will be hiring a Supervisor of Personnel to oversee the new department.

Progress Report - May, 19__

As of this date the plan to hire a Supervisor of Personnel has not come to fruition.   The dissolution of the District has created several questions which remain unanswered at this time. Hiring of new personnel is one of those questions. If we are able to move forward, I would like to interview and make a recommendation for hiring a qualified individual for the personnel department by July 1, 19___. If the position is filled by the specified date, I would hope to have the restructuring the department completed by September.

_____x_____Goal/Objective Met

_____Improvement Needed (PIP)

_____   _____
Administrator   Supervisor

_____
Date

Lower Camden County Regional High School District #1

Administrative Job Targets
School Year 19____

Category: *MANAGEMENT*

A.   **Statement of Goal/Objective:**

Establish a central purchasing/warehousing procedure

B.   **Plan:**

This year the purchasing department will be expanded to centralize purchasing of supplies, materials, and equipment. Included in the plan will be a central receiving process and the district warehouse. The district warehouse will be retrofitted and remodeled by January, 19___. Materials and supplies will be received at the warehouse starting in February, 19___. Fixed Assets will be recorded electronically and inventoried at Central Receiving

C.   **Timelines**

Some supply purchases have already been made in bulk from one vender. A cost savings has been realized already.

District Warehouse Completed - December, 19__

Materials, Supplies, and Equipment received at Warehouse - January, 19__

Fixed Assets recorded at central receiving - January through June, 19__

D.   **Progress Report - November, 19__**

After several discussions and meetings with staff, it has been determined that the fixed assets inventory will be recorded and audited by the Risk Manager. Training has already started for the Risk Manager and his secretary for recording and managing the inventory of the district's fixed assets. The change in the plan to have fixed assets recorded at central receiving was made because of a problem uncovered by the auditors when the investigated the location of items listed on the fixed assets report.

The Maintenance Department has begun their work at the warehouse. They have removed all of the old equipment from the storage area, inventoried it, and placed it in a rental truck body for a future garage sale.

Discussions have been ongoing with   our purchasing secretary, and several suppliers of materials, and equipment. We are investigating going "on-line" to order our school supplies and equipment for the 19_____ school year.

Progress Report - February, 19__

The warehouse renovation is scheduled to be completed during the Spring break. The Maintenance Department will spend the break wiring, putting in new doors, installing shelving, and upgrading the ventilation system in the garage so that it will be ready to receive supplies during the summer months. They are also remodeling the space that is to be used for storage of the district records.

Lorraine has attended several purchasing workshops and has rewritten the required pages of our bid documents. The documents reflect present State code and regulations. She has also met with the representative from   . They are developing a program which will make our purchasing/receiving more streamlined.

This management objective is on target as of this date

Progress Report - May, 19__

The warehouse has r   og   d   ,   r   since my last report.   The maintenance department worked on the re   tion   g   e spring break but did not complete the assigned task. Due to the uncertainty of   u   e   the district because of the dissolution vote I have advised the M&O Department   up on the assignment until I receive specific instructions from the Buildings and Grounds Committee.   The next meeting of the Committee will be held sometime in July and a decision will be made concerning the warehouse project at that time.

I'm disappointed that we were not able to move forward with central purchasing which I feel would have produced a substantial savings for the District.   But without a warehousing facility available it is impossible to purchase supplies in bulk.

The fixed assets inventory will be completed by a contracted service because was not able to finish the inventory before he left. The inventory will be completed by July, 19__.

_____X_____ Goal/Objective Met

_____Improvement Needed (PIP)

_____   _____
Administrator   Supervisor

Business Administrator/Board Secretary

Summary

completing her fourth year as Business Administrator/Board Secretary for the Lower Camden County Regional High School District #1.   (Name) continues to contribute to the completion of the overall mission of the Lower Camden County Regional High School District #1.

Specific accomplishments include:

1.   Successfully developing the 1999/2000 budget and having it approved by the electorate.

2.   Successful approval of a $2,750,000 lease for wiring our buildings for data, voice and video.

3.   Receiving an excellent audit evaluation of district finances.

4.   Upgrading the district comp. er   work to include E-mail, internet and intr.

5.   Successfully p.ss.   mo. t ing resulting in a seven year ce   fi   th. district.

Superintendent of Schools   Business Administrator/
                                             Board Secretary

MS:gr

cc: Personnel File

Chapter
11

Emerging Issues, Problems, Challenges, and Concepts in School Business Administration

During the past several decades, school business administrators have had to weather storm after storm of educational change. Various waves of restructuring have come and gone—and others are on their way. What can the school business administrator expect in the twenty-first century? How will schools and schooling change in the coming decades and what will be the impact on the school business function? While no one can be absolutely sure how and when the changes will occur, everyone can be sure education and support for it will be different in the future from what it is today. The current tide of educational change could dramatically alter the role of the chief business official. To assist in preparing for the future, this chapter presents six major changes taking place in education and their potential impact on the school business administrator.

Aging Population

The first Baby Boomers turned 50 in 1996. As their children leave school, this traditionally self-centered generation has begun to refocus its energy and political power on personal needs. As the generation ages, fewer and fewer adults will have any direct contact with schools. Already older Americans are reluctant to pay taxes for schooling, preferring to keep what is theirs rather than pay taxes to educate someone else's children. That reluctance will increase as our population continues to age.

In the face of continued taxpayer revolts, school business administrators will find it more and more difficult to balance the educational budget. In the coming decades, health care will continue to compete with education for public dollars. As property tax rollbacks curtail traditional sources of funds, school business administrators will have to find alternative funding sources to operate schools. Twenty-first century school business administrators will be entrepreneurs. They will have to find new funding from such widely divergent sources as foundations, investments, and selling or leasing district services and spaces for a profit. At the same time, school business administrators will have to become much more actively involved in cost/benefit analyses.

More and more, school boards and communities will look to the school business administrator for the cost perspective on educational proposals and programs. In this role, the school business administrator will provide hard cost data about the best buys in alternative instructional delivery systems and curricular offerings.

The Increasingly Pluralistic, Culturally Mosaic Society

The 1950's "Nelson" America of working dad, stay at home mom, and two white, middle-class children is gone. Minority groups are now the fastest growing segment of our population. Many school systems are finding the new student majority is Hispanic, African American, or both. This phenomenon is expected to continue well into the 21st century. In addition, between 800,000 and one million people immigrate to the United States each year. This influx of languages and cultures will drive many education policies and programs in the 21st century. The face of America is changing. School populations will reflect that growing diversity.

The mosaic composition of America will impact the business function several ways. First, political power will shift. Traditional minorities with increasing numbers will exercise growing influence in everything from electing school board members to hiring a superintendent or school business administrator. As white Americans age, and see schools taken over by those they view as different from themselves, they will be more reluctant to pay taxes. Groups traditionally supportive of education will be less so. As communities become more politically fragmented, school business administrators will find it increasingly difficult to garner wide support for tax levies and bond referenda. The cultural values and norms that Ozzie, Harriet, David, and Ricky brought to public schools will change. School business administrators will have to navigate a sound fiscal course among the various perspectives brought to schooling by people with different backgrounds and different cultures.

Continued Growth in Site-Based Management and Decentralization

The decade of the 90s saw a growing decentralization in educational decision-making. Schools have gained more responsibility for and authority over everything from the curriculum to the allocation of resources and personnel decisions. With the focus on site-based decisions, the district office is changing from central control point to resource and support system for school operations. Some school systems have even reassigned staff from the district office to the school level. Grassroots decision-making will continue to be a strong movement into the next century. In fact, some futurists picture the school of the 21st century replacing the school district of today.

The school business administrator will fill a critical role as more school system functions are decentralized. As people with little or no training get involved in business management issues, the school business administrator will be forced to be both teacher and general resource for building principals grappling with school-based budgeting, accounting systems, personnel, legal issues, environmental health, and freedom of information. The school business administrator will be a critical factor in the success of this movement—much more visible and in demand as site-based management continues to grow.

Public Education Alternatives

Many Americans believe local control for public schools is not enough. They think public education is not as effective as it should or could be. Some critics suggest that the current system needs significant adjustments. Others argue that public education should be either completely overhauled or abolished altogether. Those promoting a major overhaul propose choice among public schools, charter schools, and contracts with private companies for the operation of schools. More drastic alternatives, such as vouchers and private school choice, could promote the goals of those who would abolish the entire public school system. These alternatives are already in place in many communities. As the momentum for choice increases, schools will function quite differently. In fact, school districts may no longer exist. Those that do continue may contract out the entire delivery of education through competitive bids.

As delivery of education in America continues to move toward private sector models, the role of the school business administrator will also change. At the very least, the school business administrator could become the overseer and coordinator of contracts. Instead of managing support functions and overseeing financial and business matters related to the instructional program, the school business administrator would prepare bids, award contracts, and monitor performance of vendors who will be providing everything from classroom instruction, to foodservice, to fixed assets management. At the most, the current role of the school business administrator could cease altogether if American education moves entirely to a private choice model. Then, instead of working for a public entity, school business administrators of the 21st century could find themselves in corporate America—providing education in a competitive environment and focusing on advertising, profit margins, substantiating results, and the bottom line.

Technology and Telecommunication Explosion

Computers and telecommunications have forever changed our schools. We currently have the technology available for the world's best teachers to teach every student via television broadcasts, interactive video, Internet, and computer software. Today's students can access worldwide information on any subject without leaving their computer terminal. For many students, textbooks, paper and pencils, and worksheets are becoming a thing of the past. Instead they use laptop computers to do research, complete assignments, and read their lessons.

What will become of the school business administrator if schools exist electronically but not physically? With electronic communication, students could receive their lessons at home and come to school only occasionally to consult with teachers and classmates. Such changes would make the school business administrator's involvement in foodservice, transportation, building maintenance, and facilities planning a thing of the past. Even personnel issues could change. An increase in electronic instruction could result in fewer teachers in schools. Budget concerns would then shift from professional salaries and fringe benefits to the cost of purchasing and maintaining broadcast equipment, uplink sites, and the array of electronic tools used to deliver instruction.

The New American Culture

The biggest challenge in 21st century America will not lie in the aging population, multi-culturalism, site-based management, privatization, or technology. The biggest challenge will be leadership. Some writers have concluded that the United States has created a culture where people take positions on issues strictly based on "what's in it for me." Other writers believe that we have focused so heavily on protecting the rights of individuals that we have given little attention to what is in the best interests of the whole. Still others see a fear overtaking society that causes people to isolate themselves from each other and from institutions. Instead of getting involved in issues and discussions, people are choosing to lock themselves away with only their televisions and their computers connecting them to the rest of society. Some writers have even suggested that Americans have come to resent people in leadership roles while focusing only on their shortcomings. Americans are confident that sooner or later—sooner with the help of the media—all our leaders will fail and fall.

With this population to serve, school business administrators of the 21st century will find it increasingly difficult to lead employees and communities toward a common goal. Communication skills and knowledge of how to motivate others will be the critical elements of effective leadership. Successful school business administrators will find better ways to tie organizational goals to individual needs and desires. But success will be a two-edged sword—the more successful a school business administrator becomes, the more the public will scrutinize the position and the person who holds it. Instead rewarding the school business administrator for success, the public may attack for no other reason than selfish resentment. The outstanding school business administrator of the future will be one that has a heightened political awareness and skills—and not daunted by criticism and second-guessing.

Summary

In many respects, the role of the school business administrator in the future could be very similar to what it is today. The need for the position will continue to exist and, because of its increasing complexity, will require substantial credentials. However, in other respects the job may change dramatically—with the changes driven more by general societal forces than by innovations in budgeting, accounting, or investing.

America is rapidly becoming more diverse. Decentralization of decision-making is a fact of life. Self-interest is a driving force behind many American's views on controversial societal issues. Technology is rapidly changing all aspects of American life.

What does this all mean for the school business administrator? Quite a bit. When debates rage on educational issues, school business administrators and the knowledge they command, more than ever before, will be in the spotlight. And while technical knowledge and skill will always be the foundation for success, the school business administrator of the 21st century will need to be well versed in politics, motivation, and communication, too.

The schools of tomorrow will be different and diverse—as will be the roles and responsibilities of school business administrators. The school business administrator of the future will work in an increasingly complex world—a world fraught with ambiguity, changing political allegiances, and self-centeredness. Technical expertise will be important, but it will not be enough. Through the formal educational process, or the less forgiving school of life, school business administrators will have to learn to motivate reluctant employees, understand issues of cultural diversity, build political alliances, interact with the media,

showcase benefits versus costs of education, function in an unstable and constantly changing environment, and accurately read the prevailing winds.

Bibliography

ASBO International Resource Listing
Books for the School Business Administrator

The Association of School Business Officials International is your complete resource for information on school business administration. In addition to School Business Affairs, our magazine delivering in-depth coverage of critical issues, ASBO Accents, our newsletter covering breaking news and member activities, and the Journal of Education Finance, our peer-reviewed journal reporting the latest in education finance theory and research, ASBO publishes books designed to enhance the professional growth and development of school business officials.

From the definitive textbook on school business, Principles of School Business Management, to more narrowly focused titles, such as the School Foodservice Handbook or The New Job Description Handbook, you will find in the pages that follow, publications that will help you do your job better.

Don I. Tharpe, Ed.D.

Financial and Managerial Accounting for School Administrators
Fourth Edition

Dr. Ronald E. Everett, Dr. Raymond L. Lows, and Dr. Donald Johnson

The book that's widely acknowledged as the most respected reference on school accounting. You'll find clear, detailed explanations of financial accounting and reporting as they apply to school system fund structures. Designed as a graduate-level textbook, it also comes highly recommended for in-service programs. Whether you are new to the field or have some background in accounting, it provides a valuable resource. You'll turn to this comprehensive book again and again for information on topics such as revenue and expenditure accounting, special revenue funds, capital projects funds, trust and agency funds, internal cash control, auditing and using accounting information to measure fiscal health. 656 pages.

Stock #39 • 1996 • ISBN # 0-910170-69-X
Members: $52.50 • Nonmembers: $70

Principles of School Business Management
Second Edition

By Dr. R. Craig Wood, Dr. David C. Thompson, Dr. Lawrence O. Picus, and Dr. Don I. Tharpe

The seminal work in the field is a must-read for everyone involved in the practice and teaching of school business management. The comprehensive textbook features a broad range of topics, each meeting the diverse information needs of school administrators. Every chapter is designed to stand alone as a teaching unit or as a reference to an area of particular interest. New chapters focus on total quality management, site-based management and the future of school business management. In addition, you'll find updated coverage of all areas of school business, from strategic planning and legal liability to taxation, purchasing, budgeting, from management information systems to quantitative decision making. 936 pages.

Stock #41 • 1995 • ISBN #0-910170-70-3

Members: $52.50 • Nonmembers: $70

The New Job Description Handbook for the School Business Official

Some of the most complex jobs in school offices belong to the staff on the business side. How does one organize, staff and describe the business function in schools? This handy resource provides a storehouse of ideas you can use to write new job descriptions, revise current ones and reorganize your school district's business operations. The 1995 edition features more than 100 new job descriptions and organization charts from 50 school districts. Each is coded for enrollment and budget size, so you can compare qualifications, responsibilities and reporting hierarchy with districts similar to yours. 300 pages.

Stock #37 • 1995 • ISBN #0-910170-67-3

Members: $44.25 • Nonmembers: $59

Let's Talk School Business

By Edward Meglis, Jr., CAE, RSBA

This publication covers the topic of school business like only Ed Meglis can. It offers tips, insights and information on all aspects of the profession from someone who has seen it from all angles. Specific topics include school infrastructure, funding, budgeting and reporting, banking and investing, and much more.

Stock #13 • 1998 • ISBN #: TBD

Members: $30 • Nonmembers: $40

Internal Auditing for School Districts

By Charles Cuzzetto

If your school district implements an internal audit function, this book is for you. It is designed as a working tool with internal audit charters, policies procedures, planning and strategies laid out and explained. Over 20 sample audit guides are included providing how-to review plans for a variety of areas including: conflict of interest, risk management, record retention, budgeting, investments and more. 104 pages.

Stock #27 • 1993 • ISBN #0-910170-63-0

Members: $37.50 • Nonmembers: $50

Multimedia Budget Presentations

By Dr. Jonathan Hughes and Dr. Karl Rodabaugh

Using multimedia can make a world of difference when presenting budget information to the public or to the board. This book helps the novice get started in using multimedia applications while giving more seasoned multimedia users tips and tricks to make their presentations even better. Chapters include: "Multimedia Fundamentals," "The Graphically Thinking Business Manager," "The Effective School Budget Presentation," "On Becoming a Digital Business Administrator," and much more.

Stock #14 • 1998 • ISBN # TBD

Members: $37.50 • Nonmembers: $50

The Art of Investing School District Funds: The Rules of the Game

By Jeffrey Flynn

Learn more about the complex task of investing. Gain a better understanding of the role of brokers and areas of potential liability. This book will increase your confidence in your investment abilities by explaining the rules of the investment game. Limited quantity. 110 pages.

Stock #85 • 1990 • ISBN #0-910170-54-1

Members: $11.25 • Nonmembers: $15

Grants and Contracts Handbook

By Dr. Paul C. Holman

This is a basic reference for grant applicants, executors, project managers, administrators and staff. The ideas are school-tested and based on information gathered from institutions and agencies over the past two decades. 32 pages.

Stock #83 • 1990 • ISBN #0-910170-52-5

Members: $6.75 • Nonmembers: $9

Standards of Excellence in Budget Presentation–Second Edition

Denny G. Bolton, Ph.D., RSBA, and

W. Gary Harmer, CPA

This publication teaches readers how to develop an annual budget that meets today's most rigorous demands, using a set of budgeting guidelines created specifically for school entities. The guidelines provide a means to use the budget document as an effective decision-making and communications tool for the business management staff, school board, and community. The book contains page after page of school entity budget examples that adhere to these guidelines and have earned award recognition for their budget presentation accomplishments. If you are involved in budgeting in any way, this will be a great resource for you.

Stock #42 • 1998 • ISBN #0-910170-71-1

Members: $30 • Nonmembers: $40

How Public Schools Are Financed

By Dr. R. Craig Wood and Dr. David S. Honeyman

Help school board members, community leaders and others understand where your district gets its money and the constraints under which you operate. Written for the layperson, this concise book provides a step-by-step explanation of the philosophy and mechanics of school financing. Set of 10, 20-page booklets.

Stock #86 • 1991 • ISBN #0-910170-56-8

Members: $45 • Nonmembers: $60

Maintenance and Operations and the School Business Administrator

Here is a convenient package of information-packed articles from School Business Affairs. Covering subjects from contracting out and the environment to energy and safety issues, this highly readable collection offers you the best reading in all areas of maintenance and operations. 140 pages.

Stock #36 • 1995 • ISBN #0-910170-66-5

Members: $30 • Nonmembers: $40

School District Energy Manual

Now the rest of North America can capitalize on the highly acclaimed energy program developed by the New Jersey ASBO Facilities Committee. This comprehensive guidebook includes all the procedures and forms you need to save your school district thousands of dollars in energy costs. Topics include the business administrator's role in energy management, operations and maintenance audit for energy conservation, as well as detailed analyses of HVAC systems and maintenance schedules, building life cycle costs, and more.

Stock # 53 • 1998   New Jersey residents, please call before ordering this title

Members: $30 • Nonmembers: $40

School Foodservice Handbook

This revised guide is intended to help school administrators successfully manage their school foodservice function. It is thorough and informative, covering such topics as administration, organization, financial management, purchasing, inventory control, marketing and public communications, as well as many other issues that are associated with managing the school foodservices within your district. This all-inclusive guide is essential for those who set the highest possible standards for the school foodservices they represent. 155 pages.

Stock # 43 • 1999 • ISBN# 0-910170-48-7

Members: $14.95 • Nonmembers: $19.95

References

Everett, R. E., Lows, R. L., and Johnson, D. R. (1996) *Financial and Managerial Accounting for School Business Administrators.* Reston, Virginia: Association of School Business Officials, International.

Hill, F. W. (1960). *The School Manager: Bulletin No. 21.* Evanston, Illinois: Association of School Business Officials in the United States and Canada.

Hoy, H. K., and Miskel, C. G. (1994). *Educational Administration: Theory, Research, and Practice.* New York: McGraw-Hill, Inc.

Jordan, K. F., McKenown, M. P., Salmon, R. G., and Webb, L. D. eds. (1985). *School Business Administration.* Beverly Hills, California: Sage Publications.

Knezevich, S. J., and Dekock, H. C. (1960). Business Administration – Public Schools. In *Encyclopedia of Educational Research, III.* New York: The MacMIllan Company, 161-173.

Linn, H. J. (1956). *Are We Fit to Be School Business Administrators? Proceedings: Association of School Business Officials of the United States and Canada, 44th Annual Convention.* Association of School Business Officials of the United States and Canada.

McDuffey, C. W. (1980). *Competencies Needed By Chief School Business Administrators: A Report on the Results, Conclusions, and Implications of a Research Study to Identify the Competencies Needed by Chief School Business Administrators in Large and Small School Districts.* Park Ridge, Illinois: Association of School Business Officials in the United States and Canada.

Tharpe, D. I. (1995). *A Comparative Study of the School Business Manager's Responsibilities in School Divisions of 5,000 Students or Less in the Commonwealth of Virginia.* Unpublished dissertation. Blacksburg, Virginia, Virginia Polytechnic Institute and State University.

Urwick, L. F. (1937). Organization as a technical problem. In L. Gulick and L. F. Urwick (eds.), *Papers on the Science of Administration.* New York: Institute of Public Administration, Columbia University.

Wood, R. C., Thompson, D. C., Picus, L. O., and Tharpe, D. I. (1995). *Principles of School Business Management.* Reston, Virginia: Association of School Business Officials, International.